The SECRE EXECUTIVE SEARCH

The SECRETS of EXECUTIVE SEARCH

Professional Strategies for Managing Your Personal Job Search

Robert M. Melançon

JOHN WILEY & SONS, INC.

Published by John Wiley & Sons, Inc., Hoboken, New Jersey.
Published simultaneously in Canada.

For general information on our other products and services please contact our Customer Care Department within the U.S. at (800) 762-2974, outside the United States at (317) 572-3993 or fax (317) 572-4002.

Wiley also publishes its books in a variety of electronic formats. Some content that appears in print may not be available in electronic books.

Library of Congress Cataloging-in-Publication Data:

Melançon-Robert M.
The secrets of executive search : professional strategies for managing your personal job search / Robert M. Melançon.
    p.   cm.
Includes index.
ISBN 0-471-24415-5 (pbk. : alk. paper)
1. Job hunting.   2. Executives.   3. Management—Vocational guidance.   4. Career changes.   I. Title.
HP5382.7 .M45   2002
650.14—dc21   2002026748

Printed in the United States of America.

10 9 8 7 6 5 4 3 2 1

CONTENTS

Contents

ABOUT THE AUTHOR

Bob Melançon is the Managing Principal of Melançon & Company, a Dallas, Texas based, Retained Executive Search and Consulting firm with roots dating back to 1973 (www.MelanconCompany.com). He is also a noted speaker, writer, and author—and is widely considered an authority on the subject of executive selection.

Bob received a bachelor's degree (cum laude) in Business Administration from Loyola University with a minor in Labor Management, and holds NASD Series 6 and 63 securities licenses. Prior to entering the executive search profession, he enjoyed a highly successful corporate career in human resources management with three of the country's leading Fortune 50 corporations—Shell Oil Company, Celanese Corporation, and Frito-Lay, Inc.

In 1980, Bob left the corporate world to become an executive search consultant, and has served as the Managing Principal of his own practice for more than 20 years. He has been involved in the staffing process from all perspectives—as the candidate being recruited, as a representative of the hiring corporation, and as a search consultant serving as an agent for all parties in the recruitment process.

ACKNOWLEDGMENTS

Noted German poet, novelist, playwright, and scholar Johann von Goethe once wrote, "I owe so much to so many that if you took it all away, there wouldn't be anything left of me!"

As a young boy growing up on the Mississippi Gulf Coast, I was fortunate to benefit from the wisdom of my dearly beloved grandmother, Lorena, whose wealth of adages have proven ever more meaningful with each passing year. As I set about the task of writing this book, one, in particular, comes to mind, "Tell me with whom you associate, and I will tell you who you are" (spoken first by Goethe in 1819). All of us are but a reflection of those with whom we associate. And it has been my good fortune to be associated with the very best! It is with sincerest gratitude that I acknowledge the following for their invaluable contributions:

Dr. Donald Hanratty, Managing Partner, The Career Control Group; Richard Hardison, Practice Leader, Hardison & Company; Jack Hurst, President, Jack Hurst & Associates; Keith Nave, President, Career Management Partners; and Loren

Wells, Principal, Wells Reed Company, for sharing their friendship, professional insights, and personal experiences which has made this work so much better than it otherwise would have been.

Jim McKeen, for his insight, humor, and for giving me the opportunity to learn the search profession.

Elly Mixsell, for her communications expertise, and without whose encouragement this effort may have ended with the outline.

Michael and Melissa, my son and daughter-in-law, for their support and considerable editorial contribution.

And, most importantly, my wife, Lynell, for 30-plus years of endless support, and for sacrificing so many weekends and evenings so that I might spend them in the company of my keyboard.

Re-Engineering Your Career

Success in today's workplace demands new and innovative strategies. The traditional business model is out of sync with marketplace reality, and job security has gone the way of the buggy whip. Over 1.8 million employees lost their jobs in 2001—nearly three times as many job losses as 2000, and the highest in nine years. And with the unemployment rate now topping 6 percent, 2002 is likely to eclipse 2001! But the rotational displacement of employees is actually nothing new. According to the Bureau of Labor Statistics, nearly 700,000 job cuts were announced during 1998 for example—the peak of the economic expansion—as employers rotated out employees with "old economy" skills and rotated in employees with "new economy" skills.

Call it what you like—restructuring, re-engineering, downsizing, rightsizing, merger, acquisition—the reality is that more professionals than ever are finding themselves "in the market" for a new job. And even if you're among the fortunate who haven't been directly affected *thus far*, you probably see the writing on the wall—BRACE YOURSELF! For most of us, the days of the "gold watch," or even a ten-year job anniversary party, are gone. It has become an age of *free-agency,* and there is precious little allegiance by either employee or employer.

Job Obsolescence

The Federal Department of Labor reports that occupational half-life—the rate at which an employee's knowledge and skills become obsolete—has decreased from between 12 to 15 years in 1970, to around 30 months today. Those who are unwilling or unable to adapt or retrain will fall by the wayside. But for those who are not only able to embrace change but also harness it to their advantage, the future has never looked brighter! As Winston Churchill said: "To improve is to change; to be perfect is to change often."

Obsolete positions can translate into new opportunities for individuals with up-to-date knowledge and training. And restructuring very frequently results in new position descriptions to replace the old ones. If you know how to properly prepare and position yourself, opportunities abound.

So, even if your job has not *already left you*, there are a host of other compelling reasons why you may want to seek a new opportunity. Perhaps this explains why the average tenure for professionals has decreased from 20 years just a decade or so ago, to five years or less today.

Why Secrets *Was Written*

Ironically, many of the very best, most talented professionals are so focused on their work, and have had such little experience with the job search process, that they're actually the most poorly equipped to manage their own campaign. Because of their success, the jobs have always *found them*, rather than the other way around, and they've never had to hone their job search skills. That's why I've written this book!

This book will show you how to develop the *correct* long-term career strategy, empower you to reinvent yourself as "Me, Incorporated" for the new millennium, and teach you the techniques the pros use to identify and capture the very best opportunities, in the least amount of time, with the fewest mistakes along the way. Not just "another" position, but the *right* position, in the *right* location, for the *right* salary; the kind that you'll not find advertised in the newspaper or trade journals, or posted on the Internet. You'll discover how to think strategically about your career, and make the moves that position you like a champion.

How This Book Will Help You

The book features insider tips on how to properly package your background and experience, how to market that package most effectively, and how to separate yourself from the competition. It covers such key aspects of the job search process as:

- Networking strategies that cause the job to find you.

- The importance of coaching secondary references.

- Writing the "absolutely sure-fire, can't miss resume and cover letter."

- How to identify the key decision-makers in a target company.

- Pointers for preparing and dressing for maximum impact during the interview.

- Techniques for turning interview traps into interview triumphs.

- Little known secrets on negotiating strategy.

▌ How to handle the counteroffer.

▌ Advice for maximizing your impact during the critical first few weeks on the job.

. . . and much, much more!

Secrets is based on more than 35 years experience in human resources and executive search helping people just like you secure the best positions at the best salaries. Having held key human resource management positions at three of the country's leading Fortune 50 corporations, coupled with more than 20 years experience in executive search, I've been involved with career management from all perspectives. I'm keenly aware of how top companies go about identifying executive talent, and I know the best way to prepare and position you to capture those opportunities. I've counseled countless executives on their personal job search strategies, and I know the most effective techniques for conducting an efficient job search. I have to. That's my job, and my success as an executive search consultant depends on it!

And, to ensure that you're getting the broadest perspective possible, I've even added additional insights from several other executive search and career management experts.

Your Virtual Coach

In the absence of your own personal career management consultant, this book can serve as your *virtual coach*. Its objective is to help you work smarter and more confidently, while avoiding the mistakes and miscues that cause so many other candidates to "come in second." By putting these secrets to work on your behalf, your career will not only be destined for the right track, but also for the fast track!

I've presented the material in an abbreviated format to make it easier to use as a reference guide. But it's not only an easy read, it's a *must read* for anyone seriously considering a career move. You'll find it invaluable as you take control of your career and assume a proactive role in managing your personal job search. We'll be moving pretty fast once we get into the "secrets" themselves. But first it's important to understand how these techniques and the job search process itself, fit within the context of your overall career/life plan.

So, let's get started!

CHAPTER 1

Introspection

"If You Don't Know Where You're Going,
You Might End Up Somewhere Else"

FROM THE SEARCH FILES

"Sam" had a strong background in Corporate Finance, but had just been "released" from his third Assistant Treasurer position in the last seven years. The first two times, he assumed that the problem was with his employers. But now he wasn't so sure. Rather than initiate his typical job search "one more time," he decided to seek the help of a professional career counselor. When she asked why his previous assignments had all turned out the same, he thought for a moment, then replied, "I'm really not sure, but I know that I was extremely unhappy in all three!" The counselor then assisted him through a series of self-evaluation exercises.

Through this process, Sam realized that the duties in each of his previous positions were pretty much the same, as were the personality types of his bosses. Finally, it dawned on him that he had not really changed jobs at all. He had only changed desks!

Sam's introspection enabled him to refocus his search exclusively on opportunities offering a less structured environment, with a broader range of responsibilities, and more freedom to act. Within weeks, he accepted a position as Business Manager with a medium-sized law firm. It was just what he had always dreamed of doing, and he has now been happily employed for the past eight years.

If we're not careful we can become victims *of our experience!*

A s mentioned in the Introduction, there can be myriad reasons why you may want to find a new position. But regardless of the motivation, once you've crossed that emotional bridge, it's time to take action. For many people, this means updating the resume, making reams of copies, acquiring mailing lists, stuffing envelopes, and beginning a mass mailing campaign. But beware; it's a trap—the *activity trap*. Staying busy only makes you feel as if you're accomplishing something. You're really just spinning your wheels!

While this type of activity may lull you into thinking you're heading in the right direction, it's a false impression, and a terribly inefficient method of locating the job that's right for you. If you fall into this trap, the worst possible situation begins to happen—you start getting invitations for interviews! The more resumes you send out, the more you compound the problem. You're suddenly confronted with an internal dialogue of questions you're completely unprepared to answer. "Which interviews should I take?" "Should I entertain out-of-town interviews, or wait to see if something develops locally?" "Should I interview with company X when I really would

> **Secret #1**
>
> Beware of the activity trap.

rather work for company Y or Z?" "Could I make more money elsewhere?"

You can't properly answer these questions without first going through the extremely important process of *career/life planning*. If you ignore this step and fail to consider whether the opportunity will take you closer to or further from your career objective, odds are that you'll soon find yourself back in the process of looking for another job. A position that's just a port in a storm is very unlikely to bring you nearer the desired destination. Your career becomes like a pinball machine, with you as the ball. Bounced and bumped from place to place, you ring up a few points, set off a few bells and whistles, but eventually drop into a hole, ending the game. Wouldn't you agree that your career deserves a better strategy?

Career/Life Planning

Your occupation has a tremendous impact on your life, as well as on the lives of your family members. In his book, *If You Don't Know Where You're Going, You'll Probably End Up Somewhere Else*, David Campbell, a leading specialist in vocational testing and career guidance, writes:

> The most important influence on your lifestyle is your occupation. It will determine not only what you do every day, but it will also greatly affect how you live, who your friends are, what clothes you wear, where you take vacations, how much money you make, how long you have to work, etc. Most important, your work will have an enormous impact on how you think about yourself because we identify more closely with our occupations than with anything else.

Self-Reflection

Having an understanding of who you are as a human being, not just who you are as a professional, is critical to self-fulfillment. Embrace and appreciate your role as husband, wife, daughter, son, mother, father, neighbor, and friend, in addition to your role as an engineer, accountant, president, or CEO.

Self-reflection and analysis is key to making the right career decisions. There are numerous tools available to help you through this process, including the ever-popular book, *What Color Is Your Parachute?* by Richard N. Bolles (Ten Speed Press, 2001). You may even want to consult with a professional career management professional.

This soul-searching requires you to dig deeply into your psyche, and since it's often easier to avoid dealing with these tough questions, many people simply fall into the activity trap. In fact, it's reported that professionals spend considerably more time planning a vacation or computing their taxes than they do planning their careers. Yes, it requires a significant amount of discipline to work through this process, but there's no doubt that the effort will give you the competitive advantage.

Goal Setting

Every manager is responsible for providing direction and leadership in the accomplishment of a specific goal or objective. If you're to be an effective manager of your career, then the first step in your personal job search must be to gain a clear understanding of your long-term career/life goals. Note that I referred to the goals as career/life goals collectively, rather than as career goals and life goals separately. This is because, as stated earlier, for most of us the two are difficult, if not impossible, to separate.

The concept of managing by setting goals isn't new. Peter F. Drucker crystallized the idea in *The Practice of Management* (HarperBusiness, 1993). Since then, Douglas McGregor, Rensis Likert, and several other well-known behaviorists have also written extensively about goal setting. But perhaps Dr. George Ordiorne, considered the father of Management By Objectives (MBO), is best known for his work in this area. In his book *Management Decisions By Objectives*, Ordiorne uses MBO to measure performance against the achievement of a stated goal or objective. And it's this *"measurement"* aspect that makes MBO a particularly useful career-planning tool. Establishing long-term career/life goals provides the basis by which you can measure the appropriateness of a particular career opportunity when it's presented to you.

Another significant benefit of managing your career by goals or objectives is "self-image psychology" as described in Dr. Maxwell Maltz's book, *Psycho-Cybernetics* (1987). According to his research, the mind and the nervous system combine to form a "goal-striving servomechanism." Maltz believes that once you form a mental image of a desired goal, your mind and body will automatically do the things necessary to achieve that goal. More importantly, he found that you also will be *happier* when you have a clear understanding of your goal and can see yourself moving toward it.

By establishing career/life goals, you're much more likely to take the actions necessary to reach your long-term objectives. Determine where you want to be by a certain time in the future, and set specific goals that will help you reach your target. If you don't, you're more likely to make a mistake in your job selection, less likely to be happy in your work, and are almost certain to find your career path leading in the wrong direction. If you're working with a career management firm, you probably already have access to a number of self-assessment tools. If not, they're as close as your nearest library, bookstore, or personal computer. Use them to the fullest extent possible. When it comes to your career, an old axiom really hits home, "Those who fail to plan are planning to fail."

Melançon's Dynamic Variables (MDV)

As you work through the career/life planning process, there are three crucial career/life variables that must be prioritized before launching your job search campaign. They are:

- Time
- Dollars
- Geography

To the extent that you must be restrictive on one variable, you'll need to be that much more flexible with the others. I call this Melançon's Dynamic Variables (MDV) since each variable is influenced by the others, and all are in a state of dynamic balance. For example, if you find yourself in a situation where you need to find a new position as soon as possible, then you must be prepared to be more flexible with regard to your geographical preferences and restrictions, as well as your compensation requirements.

However, if you decide your priority is to improve your compensation, then you must be prepared to be more flexible on where you're willing to live, and how long you're willing to take to find the right opportunity. Lastly, if you wish to avoid relocation or for any reason want to focus on one particular geographical location, then you must be prepared to spend more time in the personal search process and be more flexible with your expectations on compensation. The priority you assign to each of these variables will dramatically influence the course and direction of your job search campaign.

It's extremely rare, though not entirely impossible, that you'll be able to accomplish all three objectives in a single job move. So, it's important that you come to grips with these three dynamic variables before beginning your job search. If, after weighing the choices within the framework of your career/life goals you still decide to attempt this trifecta, you'll at least do so rationally, knowing beforehand that the odds against cashing the ticket are long.

The Career versus Company Decision

Another key area of reflection is deciding whether you want to pursue a career as a professional, or with a single company. This choice also dictates very different strategies. If you choose to pursue a career as a professional, your job choices should be those that relate to a logical path in your profession. For example, if you're an Accounting Manager and aspire long-term to become a CFO, then accepting a position as a Director of Quality Assurance is not only illogical, but it's also counterproductive.

On the other hand, if you're happy working for a particular company and see the possibility of making it to the top, then accepting assignments outside of your profession for exposure and development might not only be acceptable, but also highly advisable.

Organizational Fit

When I first started in executive search, decisions about candidates were easier. They either had the required experience in a given field or they didn't. They were either a good fit for the position or they weren't. Through the years though, I've come to realize the importance of subjective factors such as corporate culture, individual personalities, and work styles. Senior-level candidates are now evaluated much more heavily on *organizational fit*, that is, how well their personalities will mesh with that of their prospective peers and superiors, whether they can support the organization's goals and objectives, and how well they will be able to conceive and articulate the organization's vision. The further they move away from their college training, the more they must rely on their management and interpersonal skills. And the more senior the executive, the more important organizational fit truly is. The good news is that everyone fits somewhere!

You can identify where you fit best by first coming to grips with who you are as a person, and then focusing on opportunities where you can maximize exposure to your strengths while minimizing exposure to your weaknesses.

Keeping Pace

It's a brave new world. As I mentioned in the Introduction, the traditional business model is out of sync with marketplace reality. There's a lack of allegiance on both sides of the desk. If you still think your employer is responsible for your future, you're in for an unpleasant surprise. In this age of free-agency, we all must be managers of our own careers.

No longer is an extended period with one employer considered a positive. In fact, it can be argued that it is actually a net negative. For one thing, merit pay increases rarely compare with the increase received when making a job change. And for another, the longer you have worked for a single employer, the more likely it is that you will have made mistakes or crossed swords politically. The fact is, many employers are more apt to fill a position with someone "from the outside" who carries no negative baggage, than to promote one of their own.

Corporations now place a premium on individuals who have worked for competitors or within a dissimilar industry. They believe the fresh perspective and stream of new ideas these individuals bring with them are competitively advantageous and essential in an environment that can quickly become stagnant without them. But be careful. Corporations say, "We want people who are risk-takers," but what they really mean is, "We want people who are risk-takers, *and always guess right!*"

We must begin to think of ourselves as *consultants* going from project to project and from priority to priority. Virtual organizations are becoming much more common, and the concept of outsourcing is growing exponentially. *Flexibility* is the key word in industry today. Corporations now bring in outside resources on a strategic basis to fill the roles traditionally held by permanent staff.

Consider this illustration:

Then: Lifetime job security.

Now: Free-agent mentality.

Then: Under five years in the same position = job hopper.

Now: Over five years in the same position = lacks ambition.

Then: Companies look for stability and tenure.

Now: Companies look for new ideas and "out-of-the box" thinkers.

Me, Incorporated

One popular approach is to look at yourself as running your own company, "Me, Incorporated," and not only are you the product, you're also the Director of Marketing, the Chief Financial Officer, and so on. You must take charge and manage your career as though it were a business. A key component of any business is its Board of Directors. The Board for "Me, Incorporated" should include mentors, professors, acquaintances from professional associations, and a few others who understand your business and the industries in which you're interested. You, as head of the company, are responsible for ensuring that you're meeting the needs of your client—your employer. You're also responsible for continually evaluating whether this is a client relationship that meets *your* needs as well as the long-range goals of your business—"Me, Incorporated."

Dr. Donald Hanratty, Managing Partner of The Career Control Group, reports that people are showing more interest in career/life planning than ever before. But he still encounters difficult cases with individuals in their late fifties who have been in the same industry and function for their entire career, who have never availed themselves of any continuing education, and who have no real network aside from a couple of tennis partners and a few neighbors. When they suddenly find themselves unemployed, it's a very difficult and distressing situation. Take steps now to ensure this picture isn't the reflection you see in the mirror.

Put It in Writing

It's not enough to just *think* about "Me, Incorporated,"—put your business plan in writing! To ensure that your career remains on the right track, your written plan should include your current compensation along with your career and compensation goals for the next five to ten years. Evaluate this document every 6 to 12 months to make sure you're progressing on target. If you're not, proactively take the steps necessary to put your plan back on track. *You*, and no one else, must take responsibility for your career.

Locked In and Turned Off

Some people find that after spending many years in the same field, they're unsatisfied or burned-out. However, they feel "locked-in" by financial commitments or other circumstances that prevent them from changing careers. Sociologists call them "locked in and turned off."

If this sounds familiar, get to work on your "Me, Incorporated" plan right away! If you're craving change and desperately seek the opportunity for a fresh start at something completely different, then your plan should carefully outline your strategy.

If you're unemployed it may be very logical for you to think, "Maybe I should consider a different field?" or, "I've always wanted to be self-employed." These aren't bad alternatives. However, the time to consider a career change is when you're gainfully employed and have numerous resources at your disposal, not when you're unemployed and emotions can cloud your judgment. No matter how turned-off you were in your last job, try to resist the temptation to change careers while you are unemployed.

Perhaps the best way to make a strategic career redirection is within your existing company. They know your track record and will be more open to a cross-functional move at a comparable salary. You'll also know colleagues who can help you make the transition successfully. It's far more difficult, if not impossible, to make a similar career change with a *new* employer. Just look at it from the prospective employer's position. Why would they want to risk paying your salary for an unproven commodity with little or no applicable experience to offer? It's a great deal for you, but a risky deal for the new employer.

Whether you're unemployed, locked in and turned off, or just considering the best way to advance, you should think of your career as a game of chess. You must formulate your strategy in advance, and then carefully consider the consequences of each move. Learn to be objective and analytical, and resist the temptation to play the first move that comes to mind. Be aggressive, but play soundly, and don't take unnecessary chances. Learn to think like a champion, and you'll soon become one.

Introspection Checklist

- ❏ Beware of the activity trap!
- ❏ Create a career/life plan.
- ❏ Set measurable goals for your career.
- ❏ Solve the MDV equation.
- ❏ Decide if your career will be "profession" or "company" driven.
- ❏ Avoid burn-out by taking the necessary steps to ensure career fulfillment.
- ❏ Recognize the job market is constantly changing.
- ❏ Manage your career as though it were a business—"Me, Incorporated."

Notes:

_____

_____

_____

_____

_____

_____

_____

_____

_____

_____

CHAPTER 2

The Reverse Search

Moving Ahead by Going in Reverse

FROM THE SEARCH FILES

One of our major clients, a CEO for a billion-dollar metals manufacturing firm, asked if I would meet with his son, whom he described as "career confused." As it turned out his son, "Charles," had actually enjoyed a fair amount of success in his career, but was burned-out and wanted a fresh start. His solution was mass mailing his resume in hopes that others would be able to figure out how he might be able to contribute to their companies. Of course, he received very little response, which only added to his disappointment and frustration.

I explained to Charles that most executives have a full-time job trying to figure out what they're *supposed to be doing, much less trying to figure out how he might contribute to their organization. Once Charles began to think like a buyer instead of a seller, and worked through the search process in reverse, he had a much better understanding of where he would fit. He narrowed his focus to just three companies, and was able to relate very convincingly how his background would benefit* them.

Within a month, he was happily employed—and now Charles is a client, too!

In order to move forward, it's sometimes best to work in reverse. Or, as Stephen Covey writes, "Begin with the end in mind."

The most effective approach for conducting your own personal search is what I call the *Reverse Search*. Note that I didn't say it was the fastest or the easiest method. Like a chess expert, you must understand that the game is not decided by how fast you play, but by carefully calculated moves that are based on knowledge of the game, as well as oneself. According to the theory of "positional chess," to take the advantage, you sometimes have to give up something in return. The same is true of the Reverse Search. The process requires self-discipline and the willingness to invest a significant amount of time and effort. However, this investment will help ensure you're the one left standing at the end of the match.

> **Secret #2**
>
> Approach your search in reverse.

Understanding the Search Process

As the name implies, the Reverse Search is the mirror image of the executive search. Therefore, it's essential to understand the executive search process before proceeding.

In its most basic form, the executive search process starts with an initial meeting, or meetings, between the search consultant and the client company to assure a thorough understanding and agreement regarding the organization, the specifications of the position, and the qualifications of the prospect sought. This may involve interviews with peers, subordinates, and superiors of the open position, including the prior employee whenever possible. Next, substantial research is conducted to collect as much information as possible on related companies, competitors, vendors, industries, functions, spheres of influence, industry leaders, and other potential resources.

Based on the data collected, the process of identifying, qualifying, and screening prospective candidates begins. Candidates are screened by phone initially and those whose experience, qualifications, and characteristics most closely match the established criteria are then personally interviewed. References, background, educational credentials, and employment history are then verified to ensure that the candidate's management ability, technical competency, integrity, and interpersonal skills are appropriate for the position, and that all relevant information is correct. Next, appropriate candidate presentation materials (candidate profile, resume, interview summary, etc.) are prepared on the leading two or three prospects for presentation to the client.

Once the client decides which candidates they wish to consider further, client and candidate meetings are arranged and coordinated. Following the initial interview(s), the client will decide which of the prospects, if any, to invite back for additional, more detailed, interviews and discussions. Should the client then wish to make an offer to one of the prospects, he will extend the offer at that point. Actually, there are many other "post-offer" steps, but these are the main ones that relate to the Reverse Search.

The Reverse Search

Now that you have some background on how an executive search is conducted, let's focus on the specific steps in the Reverse Search.

Step 1: Complete Career/Life Planning

Rather than waiting for someone to discover *you*, the Reverse Search begins with a meeting *with yourself* (and possibly your "Me, Incorporated" Board of Directors). You initiate the process by working through your career/life plan, addressing the MDV equation, making the company versus profession decision, and resolving any other issues that may remain as a result of your in-depth introspection.

Step 2: Identify and Research the Target Company(s)

Your next step is to identify those companies for whom *you* would like to work. This might be based on location, industry standing, reputation, growth opportunities, compensation practices, or whatever other criteria *you* deem important. This is a radical departure from merely sending out unsolicited resumes in hopes that someone will hire you. Now *you* are in control, and *you* are doing the selecting. Remember the MDV equation as you complete this step.

You must also find out as much information as possible about your target company(s). It's essential that you not only know your buyer (the target company), but also what your buyer is buying so you can best position what you have to sell. This should include thorough research into all aspects of the targeted company(s) including competitors, vendors, industries, functions, spheres of influence, and any other available resources. The list provided on pages 22 and 23 may be helpful in this process.

Step 3: Determine How You Can Benefit the Target Company(s)

Based on the information from your research, you must be able to make the case as to why the target company(s) should hire you. This may involve additional analysis of the company's business operations, marketing strategies, competitive environment, and so on. Ultimately, *you* must be able to demonstrate how your background and experience will solve a business problem, create a competitive advantage, or otherwise benefit the target company(s). This may well be the most important (and challenging), component of your Reverse Search. But if *you* can't make a case for why the decision-makers at your target companies should hire you given all of the research you've conducted, don't expect *them* to be able to make a case either!

Step 4: Identify the Key Decision-maker(s)

Next you'll need to identify the key decision-makers in each target company so that you can make contact at the appropriate level. This is where your earlier research will play a major role. For reasons explained later, you should target decision-makers two to three levels above the position you are seeking.

Step 5: Prepare a Resume and Cover Letter Specific to the Target Company(s)

Rather than papering the universe with generic resumes hoping hiring managers will be able to relate your background and qualifications to their needs, prepare a customized resume specific to each decision-maker, for each position sought, and for each target company.

Step 6: Forward the Resume(s) and Cover Letter(s)

Always address your resume and cover letter to a specific individual by name and title. Never use a generic, formatted, or fill-in-the-blank cover letter unless, of course, you're just trying to get rid of some old stationery. It won't be read; certainly not by the hiring manager. Mass mailings are generally ineffective and demonstrate that you lack both sincerity and ingenuity. I'll have much more to say about the do's and don'ts of resumes and cover letters in later chapters.

Step 7: Telephone Follow-up with Decision-maker(s)

Conducted properly, your telephone follow-up can be a golden opportunity to create interest and stand out to the decision-maker. More information on how best to handle telephone follow-up is included in Chapter 4.

Steps 8, 9, and 10: Initial Interview, Subsequent Interviews, and Offer of Employment

If you've put forth the effort required in the preceding steps, your results should be the same as though you were the number one candidate presented by the world's premier search firm. You can expect an initial interview, which should lead to a second or third interview, which should lead to an offer of employment. By following the Reverse Search process, you are exactly where *you* want to be—and you have been *in control* throughout the process!

The following table outlines and compares the steps in the executive search and the Reverse Search processes:

Executive Search Process	Reverse Search Process
1. Initial client meeting(s)	1. Complete career/life planning
2. Research	2. Identify and research target company(s)
3. Sourcing activities	3. Determine your benefit to target company(s)
4. Preliminary screening of candidates	4. Identify key decision-maker(s)
5. Personal interviews with candidates	5. Prepare customized resume and cover letter(s)
6. Background verification	6. Forward resume(s) and cover letter(s)
7. Preparation of resume, profile, and so on	7. Telephone follow-up with decision-maker(s)
8. Initial client/candidate interview	8. Initial interview with decision-maker(s)
9. Subsequent candidate interviews	9. Subsequent interviews with decision-maker(s)
10. Offer of employment	10. Offer of employment

Now that you understand the concept and steps of the Reverse Search, it's time to deal with the mechanics of putting your plan into action. The balance of this book is devoted to unveiling the techniques employed by seasoned executive search consultants to ensure the success of their referrals. It is not intended as a "primer" on the job search process—the assumption being that you're already acquainted with the fundamentals of resume writing, interview skills, and the like. Rather, it's an inside look at those secrets that will ensure your candidacy is positioned as positively and professionally as possible. It will also help you avoid the many pitfalls which cause other, sometimes even "more highly qualified" prospects, to fall by the wayside. Checkmate! Game over.

Reverse Search Resources

Directory of Corporate Affiliations, National Register Publishing

Directory of Leading Private Companies, Reed Reference Publishing

Directory of Executive Recruiters, Kennedy Publications

Dow Jones, Reuters, and other online information retrieval services

The Executive Recruiters of North America, Hunt-Scanlan

Guide to American Directories, B. Klein Publications

The Internet (Many companies offer extensive background and press releases on their web sites. Newspaper and magazine articles referencing your targeted company(s) can also be accessed online.)

Job Hunter's Sourcebook, Gale Research, Inc.

Job Seekers Guide to Public and Private Companies, Gale Research, Inc.

Million Dollar Directory, Dun & Bradstreet

Reader's Guide and Index to Periodical Literature, H. W. Wilson Company.

Register of Corporations, Directors and Executives, Standard &
   Poor's
Standard Directory of Advertisers, National Register Publishing
Standard and Poor's Register, McGraw-Hill
Ward's Business Directory of U.S. Private and Public Companies, Gale Research, Inc.
World Business Directory, Gale Research, Inc.

Reverse Search Checklist

- ❏ Review your career/life plan.
- ❏ Select the companies for whom you'd like to work.
- ❏ Conduct extensive research on your target company(s) and know what your buyer is buying.
- ❏ Identify how your background provides a business solution.
- ❏ Identify the right decision-maker(s).
- ❏ Prepare customized resumes and cover letters.
- ❏ Follow-up with decision-maker(s).

Notes:

_____

_____

_____

_____

_____

_____

_____

_____

_____

_____

_____

CHAPTER 3

The Resume

The Absolutely Surefire, Can't Miss Resume

FROM THE SEARCH FILES

During a colleague's search for a Regional Sales Manager, one highly qualified candidate submitted a resume on chartreuse paper with orange type and the image of a king from a deck of playing cards imprinted on each page. After my colleague stopped laughing, he called the candidate and said, "I'm just curious. What were you thinking?"

The candidate responded that he had been advised to call attention to his resume. It got attention all right, but needless to say it wasn't positive.

Unfortunately for this guy, his resume made him appear more like a joker than a king!

Your resume is much more than merely a summary of your background. It's a reflection of who you are as a person and an indication of your ability to communicate effectively. Take your resume seriously. It should be concise and clearly communicate how you've made a difference in your previous positions, along with the context in which your accomplishments were achieved.

Based on the research you've conducted on your target company(s), put yourself in the hiring manager's shoes and think through how you might be able to help him or her solve a problem or make the company more competitive. For example, consider the company's legal, competitive, cost, or marketing challenges, and highlight in your resume those aspects of your background that reflect how you've addressed similar challenges in the past.

> **Secret #3**
>
> Position
> yourself as a
> problem-solver.

Leave the lengthy novels to John Grisham and Barbara Taylor Bradford, but do write a best-seller. Your resume should be brief and easily scannable so that it instantly catches the reader's attention. Many search consultants and hiring managers receive over 100 unsolicited resumes per day and report that they initially spend no more than 15 to 20 seconds scanning each one. So, unless there's something there that immediately piques their interest, into the "circular file" it goes.

The Great Debate

Important choices in history:
> To be or not to be?
> Decaf or regular?
> Paper or plastic?

Add to that list: Reverse chronological or topical?

Experts have debated the most effective resume format for ages, and there are as many opinions as there are experts offering them. But, based on 30-plus years of experience in the field, I can tell you that there's only one surefire, can't miss resume format, and that's the one that gets you the job you want! The "right" format depends on the type and level of the position sought, the requirements of the position, and the background of the decision-maker. So, there really is no "best," one-size-fits-all, resume format. However, most veterans in the industry agree that reverse chronological is the format of preference. It's the most familiar, easiest to follow, and fastest to scan.

Topical resumes, with a host of unrelated achievements listed first, followed by a brief chronological listing of employment at the end, are the least preferable format. It begs the questions: When was the accomplishment? In what context was the accomplishment? With what staff? Over what time period? De-emphasizing your employment history by placing it at the end of your resume makes it appear as though you're ashamed of it, or you're possibly trying to hide something.

Customize and Emphasize

Always tailor your resume to the requirements of the position you're seeking. The days of mass-produced, one-size-fits-all resumes are over. By definition, a resume is an overview or summary of your background and experience. However, unless the purpose of your resume is simply to impress your mom, the

> **Secret #4**
>
> Customize each resume to the requirements of the position sought.

generic variety isn't terribly successful in stimulating interest in your ability as a problem-solver. You'll achieve far better results customizing a specific resume for each position you seek, with each target company.

Current computer technology makes customizing your resume much easier than in the past. Just save your basic, generic, all-inclusive resume in a word processing file on your computer. Then, tailor it to highlight your strengths for each opportunity, emphasizing your background in relation to the needs of the particular company. You may find that your resume looks entirely different each time you send it out. That's the point! It would be difficult to overstate the importance of customization.

Focus on Results

Resumes for entry- or lower-level positions typically highlight skills, while those for higher-level positions focus more on accomplishments or results. This is because with more junior-level candidates, their knowledge and training for the position is more relevant, and their (usually limited) experience is less relevant.

> ### Secret #5
>
> Never underestimate the importance of a well-written resume.

On the other hand, with senior-level candidates, academic training (which is probably obsolete) becomes less relevant, and managerial skills and demonstrated experience become more relevant. While you always want to stress *results* if you're at the managerial or executive level, if you possess exceptional or unusual knowledge or skills that specifically relate to the position, make sure you call attention to that as well.

It's important that you highlight not only your results, but also the context in which those results were achieved. For example, "Increased market share by 20 percent" is good, but "Increased market share by 20 percent while reducing cost of sales by 10 percent" is better. "Increased market share by 20 percent in nine months, while reducing cost of sales by 10 percent" is much better still.

Keep the Door Open

Your resume should always be a door *opener*. Therefore, take care to eliminate anything that may be construed as a door *closer*. For example, many people begin their resume with an *objective*, such as:

> OBJECTIVE: Sales or marketing management leading to a position in general management.

Think about what this conveys. A hiring manager might not even consider you for his or her Senior Product Manager position—which may be an ideal fit with your background—because it's an individual contributor position, and you stated that you wanted "management." Thus, you closed the door on that opportunity.

Or, he or she may have a position that's exactly what you're seeking, but wants someone who will be content pursuing a career in sales or marketing. By indicating that you ultimately want out of sales and marketing and into general management, once again you've effectively closed the door.

Hiring managers are most interested in what you can do for *them*, not what you can do for *someone else* down the road.

On the other hand, beginning your resume with a *summary* of your background or experience could be a good idea. Just keep it brief and unembellished. Here's an example:

SUMMARY: Senior Financial Manager with MBA, CMA and 21 years experience in strategic planning, financial planning and analysis, mergers/acquisition analysis, and systems implementations.

For some executives, an alternative may be to incorporate a *position statement* that indicates what's in it for the buyer. A *position statement* is designed to grab the reader's attention immediately, and resembles the headline in an advertisement. Here's an example:

POSITION STATEMENT: Senior Executive experienced in turning around under-performing technology-based businesses through visionary growth strategies, cost containment, and restructuring.

Don't confuse a position statement or summary with an objective. They're entirely different, and serve an entirely different purpose.

Academic Achievements

As I mentioned earlier, the goal for most hiring managers and search consultants is to scan the resume as quickly as possible to see if there's any reason to consider the candidate further. Therefore, you should structure your resume to flow in the order that's most relevant to the decision-maker. In most cases, his or her first criterion is to determine whether or not you're academically qualified for the position. Thus, it's usually wise

> **Secret #6**
>
> Orient your resume to the reader.

to have your resume reflect your academic credentials first, especially if they are a strength. If you hide them until the end, your resume may hit the round file before the decision-maker ever turns the page to learn about your Harvard MBA!

List your academic achievements with the most recent first and include dates of graduation or completion. Omitting dates is acceptable, but is less than forthcoming and may be taken as though you're trying to hide your age. Don't needlessly raise red flags or you may find the hiring manager delving more deeply into this area than he or she might otherwise have. Eventually the hiring manager will need to know the exact dates anyway in order to confirm your degrees. Age and experience are assets, not liabilities. Don't be ashamed of a few gray hairs!

Professional Experience

Following your academic achievements, list the organizations where you have worked, your dates of employment, and the positions held in reverse chronological order. Include both *month* and *year* with your dates of employment, and make certain not to leave any gaps from college to present.

Some people try using just years, instead of the month and

year format, but it's readily recognized as a thinly veiled attempt to bridge gaps in employment. For example, indicating that you worked for Company X until 1990 and joined Company Y in 1991, could mean that your employment was separated by one day, or as much as two years. You can just see the red flags popping up!

In addition to listing the *names* of the organizations where you worked, include a very brief description of each company. Never assume that the reader is aware that Company XYZ is a $2 billion, Fortune 1000 corporation that's engaged in the development of software and computer equipment. Remember, your responsibilities and achievements are only relevant as they relate to the context or environment in which you accomplished them. So, it's always a good idea to include the company's size and description. In today's marketplace, companies merge and consolidate so frequently that it's important that the reader know the type of business your company was in *at the time you held the position.*

Here are several examples:

Andersen Consulting
(An international consulting firm specializing in change management and systems implementation services.)

Apple Computer, Inc.
(An $11 billion leading-edge personal computer hardware, software systems and peripherals manufacturer.)

BMC Industries, Inc.
(A $325 million corporation with businesses in precision imaged products, focused primarily on television and computer monitor aperture masks and optical lenses.)

General Mills, Inc.
(Presently a $7 billion global food company; previously a diversified conglomerate including restaurants, toys, apparel, and specialty retailing.)

Pacific Consumer Funding, LLC
(Provides high-risk, high-rate auto loans for consumers with weak credit through its subsidiaries, NAFCO Holding Co. and Advantage Funding Group.)

Trilogy Software, Inc.
(A leading enterprise software development company specializing in front office products.)

United Companies Financial Corporation
(A $1.3 billion specialty finance company providing consumer loan products, including subprime home equity loans nationwide through 237 lending branches as well as through banks, brokers, and other lenders.)

Utilicorp United, Inc.
(An $8.9 billion New York Stock Exchange (NYSE) global energy company.)

Following each position held and a summary of the responsibilities or accountabilities of that position, list the major results or accomplishments you achieved. But make sure that they really *are* significant.

Effective Communications

The tone of your resume should be crisp and to the point. Be consistent with wording, sentence structure, style, and tenses throughout the resume. Previous experience should be in the past tense—an error often overlooked as resumes are updated. Current experience should be in the present tense. Avoid overusing the pronoun *I*.

Always use the spell-check feature of your word processing software. Remember, your resume is a reflection of who you are. Typographical errors and misspellings may give the impression that you're sloppy or careless, and could very well cost you a shot at the ideal job. However, don't rely completely on the spell-check function by itself. Carefully proofread your resume several times before mailing.

Look for misused words, misplaced plurals, grammar errors, and the like. Spell-check won't catch these types of mistakes. You don't want to have your resume read "wok" when you mean "work," unless, of course, you're seeking a position as a chef in a Chinese restaurant!

Cliché words such as, major, significant, substantial, and outstanding are subjective and should be avoided. Just clearly state the facts and let the reader be the judge as to just how significant the accomplishment was. Overselling can be just as bad as underselling.

The Importance of Action Words

Use tangible action words to describe your experience. The following list illustrates a variety of words that will make a positive impact when used appropriately.

Accomplished	Facilitated	Obtained
Achieved	Formulated	Performed
Built	Generated	Produced
Conducted	Headed	Reduced
Controlled	Implemented	Resolved
Coordinated	Improved	Restructured
Designed	Increased	Served
Determined	Managed	Supervised
Developed	Marketed	Wrote
Expanded	Negotiated	

Beware of Jargon

It's easy to get caught up in industry jargon. Again, you should write the resume for the benefit of the reader. Unless you're absolutely sure who that will be and what his or her background is, it's best to try to avoid industry jargon and buzzwords. Clear communication is critical. Spell out all abbreviations on first reference. You can then use the abbreviation later, if necessary. For example, when referring to your experience with Ernst & Young, write Ernst & Young (E&Y) on first reference, then simply use E&Y later. When referring to your affiliations, write International Association of Business Communicators (IABC). IABC will suffice thereafter.

Secret #7

Make sure
you're perfect
in print.

35

Other Resume Tips

▪ Don't try to cram too much onto a page. Effective use of white space is pleasing to the eye, enhances the overall look, and makes the resume easy to scan.

▪ As a courtesy to those of us over 50 years of age, don't make the type so small that we need a magnifying glass to read it! Keeping the resume brief doesn't mean including excessive information, only in smaller print.

▪ Use standard $8\frac{1}{2}$" × 11" sheets of paper. White, ivory, or very pale gray in linen or laid finishes are good choices. Crane's 32-pound resume paper is a favorite of many.

▪ Each copy of your resume should be an individually printed copy. Don't send out photocopies, or use a dot matrix printer. For this task, a laser or ink jet printer is essential. If you don't have one, there are many companies that provide this service.

▪ It's a good idea to do a test to see in what condition your resume arrives. Often, when you fold resumes and the U.S. Postal Service processes them, the print smudges or pops off along the folds, making it both unattractive and difficult to read. Before sending your resume to target employer(s), mail a copy to yourself. This will enable you to correct any problems and ensure your resume arrives in the condition intended.

▪ Don't use colored paper, sketches, cartoons, or oversized paper. These get attention all right, but it's the wrong kind of attention. Also, remember that many types of colored or mottled paper cannot be copied or faxed without making the resume unreadable. And, please, no chartreuse paper!

Avoid Getting Too Personal

Again, resumes should be door openers, not door closers. You generally have more to lose than to gain by including irrelevant information. So, get personal only when it's to your advantage. However, if your avocational interests or hobbies could be seen as a strength, then you very well may want to include them. For example, if you're a "seasoned" professional, the fact that you run marathons or play tennis competitively will help dispel any notion that you might not have the energy to do the job.

If you're applying for a position in sales or marketing, you might want to include avocational interests that relate to your sociability, such as golf or school board chair. If you're seeking a position in information technology, your participation on a chess team or your computer-building hobby will be a plus.

It's generally recommended that you omit irrelevant personal data such as marital status, height and weight, and so on. But here again, if you feel this is an asset, you may want to include it. Of course, you'll want to include your professional or trade association affiliations, if they're appropriate to the position sought.

Some other common door closers that seldom help, but frequently hurt are:

- Religion
- Childcare issues
- Political affiliation
- Salary requirements
- Unrelated personal data

- Unrelated hobbies
- Disabilities/limitations
- Travel restrictions
- Geographical restrictions
- Any restrictions

E-Resumes

According to *Investor's Business Daily*, in the digital age your resume may not be worth the paper it's printed on—it's worth a lot more. The Internet has changed the way job seekers present their credentials. Technologically savvy job applicants are now using electronic resumes. These e-resumes are similar to their "paper cousins," and are used to apply for jobs via e-mail or on web sites.

If you have professional papers, video, art, work samples, or computer programs to showcase, a personal web page may be a good way to go. The web site also allows prospective employers to view your portfolio, and access detailed information about you without shuffling through a mountain of paper.

The experts say that digital self-promotion is increasingly important for job hunters, and that going digital is more efficient and effective than traditional paper and ink. For one thing, e-mail is lightning fast, allowing employers to respond more quickly, and sort through resumes using computer technology.

So, since many companies welcome or even require electronic copies of your resume, be sure to have an e-mail version ready to go. If you plan to send the document as an e-mail attachment, be sure to create it in a widely accepted word processing software format, such as Microsoft Word. But keep in mind that while later versions of MS Word can read .doc files created by earlier versions, earlier versions of MS Word cannot read .doc files created by later versions! You should also be aware that unusual fonts, special characters, italics, underscoring, bold facing, or other exotic formatting may get distorted or even omitted during transmission. This is especially true when the receiver is using a different version of software than the sender. The same potential exists when hard copy resumes are scanned into resume databases; a pretty standard practice at most companies these days. Keeping the formatting straightforward will help in both regards.

Some experts recommend avoiding attachments all together since they may get garbled en route, deleted, or ignored. Instead, they recommend copying and pasting your resume and cover letter into the body of an e-mail message. It's a good idea to send a copy of your e-resume to a friend who uses a different e-mail program and/or Internet service provider before sending it to a potential employer. This will allow you to see how your e-resume will look when it reaches its final destination. Simply e-mailing a copy to yourself is of little benefit since the e-mail will go out and return through the same ISP gateway. The problems occur, if there are any, when the e-mail passes through two or more *different* gateways.

Think Keywords

Employers and recruiters often search electronic resume databases using keywords. To ensure your e-resume turns up as a match, it should include terms and phrases that indicate your expertise. The keywords tend to be *nouns* reflective of the skills, hot-button terms, and experience employers may be seeking. This differs from the importance of using *verbs* in the printed version of your resume.

These keywords should be listed in a *keyword summary* on the top of your resume just under your name and contact information. Basically, a keyword summary is a listing of all the words (nouns) or phrases that a prospective employer might use in his or her electronic search. For example, if you are a Network Engineer your keyword summary might look like this:

> Keyword Summary: Network Engineer. Network Specialist. Network Analyst. Systems Analyst. LAN/WAN. TELECOM. MIS. Radio/Video. Novell IntranetWare. Microsoft NT4.0 Workstation & Server. Exchange 5.5. SQL 7.0. WIN95. WFW311. DOS. MAC-OS. Routers. Bridges. Hubs. Protocol Analysis. Bandwidth Analysis. Programming. Mainframe and network integration. Project management. Client/server. Client/network systems analysis. C. C++. COBOL. FORTRAN. ASSEMBLY. UNIX.

(Note: Unlike hard copy resumes, industry jargon, acronyms, and so on are okay in e-resumes since decision-makers may also conduct their electronic search using these terms as keywords.)

Some candidates fail to recognize that hard copy resumes actually become e-resumes once they're scanned into a resume database. For this reason, it's a good idea to include a keyword summary in the hard copy version of your resume as well. But place it at the end of the resume so it will be less distracting.

> **Secret #8**
>
> Include a keyword summary in your hard copy resume.

The statistics make a compelling case: 60 percent of the world's 500 largest companies now advertise positions on their own web sites, and more than 200,000 web sites focus on some aspect of recruitment. Don't overlook the value and increasing importance of the Internet as you conduct your job search.

Just the Facts

Even if you're less than proud of your achievements, resist any temptation to embellish your qualifications. Always be honest. Don't stretch the truth. Dishonesty is not only wrong, but it also could lead to your failure on the job, or even be cause for dismissal.

Resume Don'ts

▌ Don't indicate, "Willing to Travel" on your resume. Most hiring managers assume this of professionals. If you're unwilling or unable to spend time on the road, address that during the interview, after the company has fallen in love with you and your qualifications. Your positive attributes may outweigh your inability to travel.

▌ Don't include, "References Available Upon Request." This is obvious!

▌ Don't include a photo with your resume unless asked to do so—it is considered unprofessional.

Resume Checklist

- ❏ Your resume is an extremely important document. Treat it as such.
- ❏ Customize every resume.
- ❏ Use the reverse chronological format.
- ❏ Focus on results.
- ❏ Eliminate door closers.
- ❏ Have an electronic version of your resume ready to go.
- ❏ Double-check for errors.

Notes:

_____

_____

_____

_____

_____

_____

_____

_____

_____

_____

_____

_____

CHAPTER 4

The Cover Letter

Exposing Yourself!

FROM THE SEARCH FILES

While I was conducting a search for the semiconductor division of a multibillion dollar international electronics firm, the division President related the story of a young engineer who "accidentally" ran into his car in the parking lot. The engineer was most apologetic and insisted upon taking personal responsibility for handling everything relating to the accident including the claims process, the repairs, seeing that the President (then a Vice President of Operations) had a car to use while his was in the body shop, and so on. Through the process, the two became quite friendly, and the President was highly impressed by the engineer's "take charge" approach.

Years later, after the engineer had advanced to Director of Operations reporting directly to the President, he confessed that the accident was no accident. He deliberately ran into the President's car in order to stand out from the thousands of other engineers, to get to know the President on a personal level, and to demonstrate his managerial skills.

While the young engineer's strategy was successful, there are better, and less risky, ways to get noticed!

Never forward a resume without a personalized cover letter. To underestimate the potential of a well-thought-out and well-written cover letter is to miss out on a key opportunity to call attention to your candidacy. Like the resume, your cover letter should demonstrate how you can benefit the company, help solve a particular business problem, or capture a specific business opportunity. But whereas the purpose of your resume is to summarize your qualifications, experience, and accomplishments, the purpose of your cover letter is to create a compelling reason for the decision-maker to *want* to review your resume.

> **Secret #9**
>
> Promote yourself with the cover letter.

It represents a golden opportunity to demonstrate your creativity, knowledge of the target company's business, ability as a communicator, and, in general, *stand out* from the hundreds of other candidates. Once again, your earlier research will pay major dividends in this regard.

How to Write It

Your cover letter should create interest and augment, not merely restate, your resume. It should be extremely brief—never more than a couple of short paragraphs—and have a central purpose or theme. Decision-makers will quickly scan only the first sentence or two to see if there's any reason to read further, so you only have about three to five seconds to catch their attention and make an impact. If a specific individual has referred you, someone whose name may have a positive impact with the decision-maker, be sure to mention it up front. This is one of the fastest and most effective ways to get attention. But don't lie. It will eventually be uncovered, and then it will work against you.

Where to Send It

You should address the cover letter to a specific person by *name and title— spelled correctly.* Mass mailing your resume is not only ineffective, but it can also be counterproductive. Your goal is to separate yourself from the competition, not merely blend in to the crowd.

Secret #10

Make contact two or three levels above the position sought.

Never begin a cover letter with, "To Whom It May Concern," or, worse still, "Dear Sir." You can just bet that Ms. Jones, the Vice President of Finance and your prospective boss, will take that one to the shredder personally. Lastly, don't insult the reader by using a form letter approach where you *write in* the addressee's name on the blank line!

Aim High

Target the executive two to three levels above the position in which you have an interest. There are several reasons for making contact at this level:

■ The incumbent in the position (if there is one) is certainly not going to recommend hiring you if he or she sees you as a threat.

■ The boss of the incumbent in the position you're seeking may be in trouble also, and the last thing he or she wants is to have a potential replacement on board. By going a level above your boss, you'll give your boss' boss the opportunity to bring in a potential replacement.

■ The higher the level of the person you contact, the more likely someone will act on your resume when it's passed down.

■ Senior-level executives frequently *create* positions. You may fit a position that he or she has been thinking about creating, but hasn't yet discussed with other staff members or human resources.

Aim Correctly

While Human Resources is a highly professional and vitally important strategic partner in most organizations, it's usually far more effective to contact the decision-maker(s) directly. In some cases, human resources may not yet be aware of a potential opening, or other, perhaps more senior-level opportunities for which you may be qualified. In addition, staffing responsibilities are often delegated to the least senior professional in the human resource organization. Occasionally, these individuals may lack the creativity and business savvy necessary to make the translation as to how your (perhaps seemingly unrelated) experience fits the job requirements. Again, some degree of spadework may be necessary to identify the right decision-maker, but you *can* do it. Executive search consultants do it every day.

When you do make contact with the decision-maker, don't ask if there are any openings. That's an invitation for a very short conversation. Remember, decision-makers have the power to *create* positions when they find someone they want on their team—whether an opening exists or not—and they often do.

What's in It for Them?

Decision-makers are primarily interested in how you can make *their* job easier, how you can make *them* look better, and how you can make the company more successful, usually in that order. So, always make sure you convey how your background and experience will benefit them personally. Too many cover letters start off by stating why the *candidates* are seeking to make changes, why *they* lost their jobs, why *they're* interested in the company, or other things pertaining to *themselves*. What they should be doing is emphasizing what they can do for the *decision-maker* or the *company*.

> **Secret #11**
>
> Appeal to the decision-maker's self-interest.

> **Secret #12**
>
> Knowing the "code" will give you the advantage.

Breaking the Code

Like most other professions, there's a *secret code* search consultants and decision-makers use, which enables them to sort through reams of letters and resumes in a matter of minutes. By knowing the code, you can use its translation to your advantage. Here's an example of how it works:

If your cover letter opens:

Then the translation is:

"I am a results-oriented _____, with a proven track record. . . ."

"Nothing to offer . . . NEXT!"

"Enclosed is a copy of my resume for your review. . . ."

"Master of the obvious . . . NEXT!"

"Could you or one of your clients use a. . . ."

"Desperate . . . NEXT!"

Perhaps worst of all is:

"Your organization was referred to me as one that may have an interest in reviewing my credentials for. . . ."

"Hi, I'm lazy, have no creativity, no imagination, know nothing about your company, I'm working with an outplacement firm, and I'm mass mailing my resume in hopes that someone—anyone— will hire me. Any interest? . . . NEXT!"

Needless to say, these cover letters, along with the resumes accompanying them, move at light speed into the *black hole* known as the circular file.

Now, here are some examples of more professional, personalized opening paragraphs that will make a far greater impact, and will be far more likely to result in a decision-maker reviewing the writer's resume.

> Dear Mr. (or Ms.) Decision-Maker: I was speaking with George Brown, your Vice President of Logistics, about XYZ Corporation's renewed focus on quality assurance, and he suggested that I make you aware of my experience as an ISO9000 Team Leader with Widgets, Inc.

Or, even better (because it's briefer):

> Dear Mr. (or Ms.) Decision-Maker: George Brown suggested that I make you aware of my 18 years experience as a Quality Assurance Team Leader.

Since the decision-maker isn't sure about the writer's relationship with George, he or she will normally spend at least a few minutes reviewing the resume, just in case George should ask about it. Another example, based on the research you conducted, might be:

> Dear Mr. (or Ms.) Decision-Maker: I noticed in *Widgets Daily* that XYZ Corporation will be joint venturing with Programmers Galore, Inc. to further penetrate the software development market. No doubt this venture will also position XYZ as a dominant player in systems integration. But, to take full advantage of the opportunity, you'll likely need a Senior Software Development Manager with experience in technology conversion. My background includes. . . .

In a just a few short sentences you have: (1) demonstrated to the decision-maker that you're in tune with his or her business and marketplace; (2) conveyed that you're insightful, innovative and creative; (3) proven that you're willing to do the extra research that others aren't; and (4) made the case for how you can help him or her solve a business problem and take further advantage of business opportunities.

You Asked for It

Should you be responding to an advertisement, Internet posting, or other situation where you know the criteria for the position, one highly effective approach is a two-column, "You Asked For—I Have" cover letter. Here's an example:

You Asked For:	I Have:
Engineering degree, with advanced degree preferred	BS in Mechanical Engineering with master's degree in Business Administration
Minimum of 12 years experience in electronics or related industry	15 years experience in electronics, robotics and systems integration
Managerial experience	Managed a staff of 52 and 50 in my last two positions, respectively
Knowledge of computer-based engineering systems	Worked extensively with various manufacturing systems including:

	ESD simulation, LSAR, CDR, ORLA, ASIC design, and so on
Bilingual skills	Fluent in English, Spanish, and German
Willingness to relocate to the Dallas, Texas area	Presently live in Plano, Texas (suburb of Dallas)

Properly executed, this can be an effective, easy-to-read approach that is brief, unusual, and will help you stand out from the rest.

Keep It Clean

It's best to use personalized stationery and envelopes for your cover letter, preprinted with your name and address—no shields, coat of arms, cartoons, and so on. Ideally, the paper should be slightly smaller and of a slightly different color than the resume. Monarch $7\frac{1}{4}" \times 10\frac{1}{2}"$ is a good choice. Remember that dark-colored or mottled papers don't copy, scan, or fax well.

Carefully review your letter for typographical errors and misused words. Your letter should be cordial and error free. Of course, *never* use your current employer's letterhead. Customized cover letters, demonstrating that you're serious enough to have done your homework and highlighting how you can benefit the company, will give you a powerful advantage over your competition. It's an extremely important component of your overall strategy to direct and manage your career.

Follow-up Calls

Indicating in your cover letter that you're going to follow-up with a phone call in a few days can sometimes be very effective. Most decision-makers will take a few extra minutes to review the resume so they can respond intelligently when you call. But if you say you're going to follow-up, be sure to do so, and call at the designated time. If your schedule is such that you might not be able to phone at a specific time, you can still make a follow-up call, just don't indicate in advance that you will do so on a certain day or at a certain time.

For senior-level positions, executive assistants will most likely screen you out, but the decision-maker will at least get a message that you called as you indicated that you would. On the other hand, you just might get through to the hiring manager. If so, it's a great opportunity to sell yourself. Be mindful of the hiring manager's time and be sure you have a strong benefit to offer. Your call might go as follows:

> Hi, Bill. My name is Joe Smith. I don't know if my name rings a bell, but I'm Vice President of Finance with Widgets, Inc. in Detroit. Perhaps George Brown, your Vice President of Logistics, mentioned my name. I was speaking with George at the Financial Leadership Conference last month, and he said that you might need a CFO to direct XYZ's planned acquisitions in the software development market. I just thought I would follow-up to be sure you received the resume I forwarded last week, and offer to answer any questions that you might have.

Notice that the caller didn't ask a question, but rather gave an explanation of the purpose for the call, made a brief mention of the company's business opportunity, and referred to his qualifications.

Your Hotline to Success

While conducting your job search, think very seriously about adding a second dedicated telephone line with a professional voice mail service. There are several reasons why this is important.

> ### Secret #13
>
> Install a dedicated second phone line with voice mail.

- ▌ Humorous messages on your answering machine may have their place, but not in the job search.

- ▌ As cute as your toddler may be, when he or she answers the phone and it's the Vice President of Operations calling, you're immediately positioned in a less-than-professional light. In fact, you may never even get the message that he or she called!

- ▌ When a senior executive calls from aboard the Concorde en route to London, you'll be glad your voice mail picks up 24-hours-a-day.

- ▌ Even the most responsible teenagers are notorious for spending hours on end tying up the telephone line. Missed calls equal missed opportunities.

- ▌ Computer modems are also responsible for missed calls if they share the same line as your telephone.

Here's a real-world example that illustrates the point. "Joe," a friend and colleague, once placed a Vice President of Acquisitions with a large, diversified industrial manufacturing company in the Midwest. Several years later, "Ralph," the former candidate, called my colleague to say that he had been unemployed for some time and wanted to see if there was anything Joe could do to help him. After giving it considerable thought my colleague called Ralph back to offer a few suggestions.

Day after day, however, for hours on end, Joe got nothing but busy signals.

Finally when he did get through late one evening, he found that Ralph had one phone line, and since he was unemployed, he spent all day doing research connected to the Internet. Despite Joe's admonition to the contrary, Ralph still has the one phone line and still conducts research on the Net all day. He's been unemployed going on two years now, and he wonders why!

Cover Letter Checklist

- ❏ Personalize your cover letter.
- ❏ Be brief.
- ❏ State your benefits.
- ❏ Augment the resume.
- ❏ Use good-quality, light-colored paper.
- ❏ Follow-up at the designated time.
- ❏ Install a dedicated telephone line for your job search.

Notes:

_____

_____

_____

_____

_____

_____

_____

_____

_____

_____

_____

_____

_____

CHAPTER 5

References

Coaching the Coach!

FROM THE SEARCH FILES

"Mary" is a professional acquaintance of mine. She had been on the job market for several months when over dinner one evening she asked if I might be able to give her some advice as to "what she was doing wrong." It seemed that her job search had pretty much settled into the "always a bridesmaid, never a bride" syndrome. She made an excellent appearance, had two advanced degrees, very substantial experience in public accounting, a well-drafted resume, and, on the surface, seemed to be doing everything right. As a courtesy, I offered to check her references to see if there was something I was missing.

The first reference responded that all he would verify was her dates of employment (a kiss of death). The second reference began with, "I can't believe Mary would give my name as a reference." And that was the most positive thing he had to say! There was no need to go any further.

Mary had "assumed" that because she had worked with these managers for several years, they would give her a positive reference. But, had she bothered to check with them in advance, she would have known just how happy they were to see her leave.

Before accepting an invitation for an interview, make sure you have your references lined up, and that you know what each of them will say. Always ask references in advance for permission to use their names. It's also a good idea to give them a heads-up each time you offer their names as references. They should never be surprised by calls from your prospective employers.

References can make or break your candidacy, so leave nothing to chance. Make sure all of your references have a copy of your resume and that they are very familiar with the entire scope and breadth of your background. In addition, be sure to give them a solid understanding of the position you are seeking. The more they know about you and the job under consideration, the better prepared they'll be to communicate the desired information.

> **Secret #14**
>
> Be sure you know what your references will say.

Don't include a list of references with your resume. You may well participate in several rounds of interviews with several prospective employers, and your references will not appreciate being called repeatedly. References are an extremely important asset in your campaign, so use them sparingly and be considerate of their time. If asked, simply explain to the interviewer that you'll be happy to provide a list of references once you've determined your level of interest in the position, or as soon as you are deemed a finalist for the position. Of course, you'll want to convey this in a very positive and professional manner so you don't appear evasive.

Five or six references are usually adequate, but offer more if possible. Most decision-makers are only interested in professional references. Personal references such as clergy, neighbors, or family members are much less relevant. After all, what would personal references have to say about your qualifications for the position? That you attend church regularly, mow your lawn, or make a wicked lasagna?

Former bosses always serve as the strongest references. Offer them when you've enjoyed good relationships and feel confident that they'll give strong reports of your abilities. Another highly positive gesture—depending on your circumstances—is to offer your current boss, former bosses, or other professionals at your *current* company. This shows you have nothing to hide. However, if you're still employed, be very cautious about offering such references as it could cost you your job. A safer approach is to provide these references only when a company is prepared to make you a firm offer of employment, or has already extended an offer contingent upon satisfactory references.

The Reference Loop

A technique that can be particularly helpful is called "closing the loop on references." Frequently, the reason why candidates don't get invited for a final interview is because of weak or mediocre references. Hiring managers will often ask your listed references for the name of another person familiar with your work *who isn't on your list*. So, you should ensure that your primary refer-

---

Secret #15

"Close the loop" with your references.

ences have the names of one or two other individuals to refer—individuals that you've also prequalified and coached. These secondary references should all be positive and enthusiastic about your background and experience. Try to ensure that each one is prepared to mention a different strength or attribute.

Once the interview process is concluded, be sure to call or write and thank each reference for their time and courtesy. Again, they are an extremely important asset and should never be taken for granted.

A Graceful Exit

Because of the importance that references can play in the overall success of your career, always try to leave your current employer with your bridges intact. When departing, your exit should be handled gracefully and professionally no matter how you actually feel about your boss or the company. You never know what role these potential references may play in the future!

References Checklist

- ❏ Provide references only when you're a finalist for a position.
- ❏ Ask references in advance for their permission to use them.
- ❏ Offer only professional references.
- ❏ Former bosses can be strong references, but use caution.
- ❏ Provide all references with a copy of your resume in advance.
- ❏ Coach your references on your strengths.
- ❏ Don't forget to "close the loop."

Notes:

_____

_____

_____

_____

_____

_____

_____

_____

_____

CHAPTER 6

Preparing for the Interview

Featuring—You!

FROM THE SEARCH FILES

A colleague referred a candidate to interview for a Vice President of Human Resources position. He met with two senior-level executives, and they both liked him a lot. He was then invited to interview with the Chief Executive Officer. As the candidate sat down, the first thing out of the CEO's mouth was, "I've never been very impressed with your current employer. In fact, I've not been even mildly impressed with anyone who works there. Why don't you take a minute to tell me how you're different from all the bozos you work with?"

The candidate later asked my colleague, "What would you have done?" He responded that he would have closed his briefcase and said, "You look like a busy guy, and I've got some things to do myself, so why don't we see if your Secretary can get me on an earlier flight and not waste a lot of each other's time."

Be prepared for anything during the interview!

Congratulations! You successfully showcased your accomplishments in your resume and created enough interest through your cover letter that you've been invited for an interview. Well, enjoy the moment, but don't break out the champagne just yet. One of the most important parts of the job search process is at hand.

The Sales Process

Most people think that their role as an interviewee is passive—remaining conscious during the interview, responding to the interviewer's questions when asked, and trying to avoid mistakes. These are the people who seldom ever make it past the initial interview. In fact, you have some pretty important responsibilities as an interviewee and must be prepared to play an active role in the process. The interview is where you *sell* yourself to the decision-maker. And like every other sales situation, there are proven techniques that can significantly enhance your chances to close the sale.

> **Secret #16**
>
> Use features and benefits to make the sale.

Features and Benefits

Many years ago, a premiere international photocopier company developed an approach to personal selling skills which has proven to be enormously popular. It has been so successful, in fact, that it's considered the standard in the industry. In essence, the technique involves first understanding what the customer is *really* looking for, then demonstrating the *features* of the product or service, followed by an explanation of how that feature will *benefit* the buyer. Thus, the technique has become known as "selling features and benefits."

To illustrate this approach, let's say you're in the market for a new vehicle. What you really want is something that will comfortably and safely accommodate you, your spouse, and your two small children. As you walk into the first showroom, the salesperson approaches you and proceeds to tell you all about the company's newly redesigned sportscar, which seats two, will do 0 to 300 mph in four seconds, has a convertible top, is on sale "today only" for just $80,000, and comes with a matching picnic basket. Not only has he turned you off, but he has also wasted your time and lost the sale to boot.

When you arrive at the second showroom, the sales representative welcomes you and asks you what you're looking for in a car. She knows that only after she understands your real *need* can she proceed to help you satisfy that need. After carefully listening to your requirements, the representative takes you to the dealer's latest model minivan and describes how the features of the van provide the benefits you seek.

She shows you how the back doors open on both sides—the feature—and explains that the kids will be able to get in and out easily—the benefit. She continues describing the vehicle's sturdy frame—the feature, and how comforting it will be to know your family will be well-protected in the event of an accident—the benefit. Lastly, she demonstrates the spacious cargo area—the feature, and subtly helps you envision transporting your kids' sports gear, not to mention your golf clubs—the benefit.

Now, begin thinking about your credentials, skills, experience, background, and anything else you have to offer in terms of features and benefits. Picture yourself as a product and the decision-maker as the customer. Identify what your customer's needs are, and how you can satisfy those needs by first highlighting the features of your background, and then explaining how they will benefit the employer—your customer.

Carpe Diem

Remember that just as the best qualified candidates are often the most poorly equipped to manage their own job search, highly placed decision-makers are frequently the poorest interviewers. But even if they have failed to obtain proper or sufficient information, they will still make a decision following the interview. And, once made, their decision is typically irrevocable. Over and over, candidates return from interviews to report that the hiring manager spent the entire time talking about the company, and asked very few pertinent questions. When this happens, it's just a matter of time before I get a call from the hiring manager saying that the company has no further interest—because the candidate *wasn't qualified!*

When appropriate, it's imperative that you take the initiative to find out what the decision-maker (buyer) is buying and sell him or her on the features and benefits of your experience—even if it means *volunteering* information about which you were not specifically asked. The onus is on *you*, not the decision-maker, and it's critical that you seize the opportunity.

Here's a scenario: Your research indicates that the company with whom you're going to interview is considering entering the paging technology market. Don't *assume* that the decision-maker will pick up on your experience in this area from your resume. Rather, make your case by describing your background in the paging industry (feature), and explaining how that experience would be applicable to the company's situation (benefit). For example, you might say: "It may not be obvious from my resume, but while I was Director of Business Development for Widgets Inc., I was responsible for directing our mergers and acquisition efforts, which included the acquisition of PagersRUs, Inc. I would think that my six year's experience in this area could be of significant value in helping XYZ ramp-up very quickly in this new technology, should you decide to pursue that market."

Just as chess champions know that they must constantly be alert to any opportunity to seize and maintain control of the board, successful candidates know they must take control of the interview and direct the conversation toward their background and the benefits they offer. For instance, when the hiring manager references a business problem he or she is facing, use that to your advantage by saying, "We had a similar problem at my company, and here's how I handled it."

Research, Research, Research

The extensive research you conducted into the target company(s) prior to drafting your resume and cover letter will also go a long way in helping you prepare for the interview. You should be ready to provide concise, yet complete, answers to the interviewer's questions, and to ask intelligent, meaningful questions of your own. Well-thought-out questions are taken by the interviewer as an indication that you have a serious interest in the company and have taken the time to do your homework. Thoroughly analyze your experience in the context of what you know about the company, and be prepared to communicate how your experience relates to the hiring manager's needs.

Keith Nave of Career Management Partners, and past President of the Dallas/Fort Worth chapter of the International Association of Career Management Professionals suggests, "When interviewing, the most important thing is to be yourself; the second most important thing is to be prepared. And the more prepared you are, the more you can relax and be yourself!"

The more you know about the target company, the higher your odds of success. If possible, you should know the company's products, services, organizational structure, culture, customers, competitors, parent company, subsidiaries, principal locations, industry standing, sales/revenues, market share, historical growth, and so on. This information is readily available through the Internet, annual reports, trade publications, library reference departments, stockbrokers, and the like. All you have to do is look. This will give you a great deal of confidence and a competitive advantage over the other "players."

One highly effective approach for gaining additional insight into the target company and decision-maker is to contact current or former employees of the firm. Even in large cities, it's not too difficult to find someone who used to work at any given company. Vendors, suppliers, and individuals working at competitor firms can offer some valuable input as well. Your networking and professional/trade association involvement will be an asset here, too. Try to find out about the corporate culture and the background of the interviewer if you can.

Know Thyself

The interviewer will be looking for a history or track record of success. He or she may want to go back as far as high school, so be ready with examples of your achievements.

How did your leadership and teamwork skills make an impact on the success of your school's softball or football team? If you were involved in a fraternity or sorority in college, describe how you handled the finances as treasurer, or successfully directed the fund-raising campaign for a new fraternity house.

Of course, your more recent accomplishments are the most important. Whenever possible, you should respond to questions by using a current or recent example. Be thorough and complete, but don't go off on a tangent. Think about the achievements of which you're most proud and be ready to explain them using specific examples. Adopt a "we" approach and position your responses as though you are already part of the team.

It's not enough to say that sales in your department increased 15 percent when you were Sales Manager at XYZ Corporation. Relate how *your specific involvement* contributed to the increase rather than vague generalizations such as, *we* did this, or *our department* was responsible for that. But don't go overboard and appear too "me-focused." You won't want to come across as though you were a quarterback without a team. Companies always want to employ people who can work well with others.

Many interviewers work from the premise that past behavior is the best predictor of future behavior. So, take advantage of this knowledge and weave together a track record of solid achievements. You should know your background, dates of employment,

> **Secret #17**
>
> Be intimately familiar with all aspects of your background.

and record of accomplishments backward and forward. *Never* refer to your resume during an interview.

Responding to Questions—The Melançon Formula

Here's a formula I frequently recommend to ensure your answers are clear, succinct, and complete:

<table>
<tr><td>

Secret #18

Use Melançon's Formula to provide a thorough response.

</td><td>

1. State the problem or challenge.

Example: Production was down 40 percent because of a shortage of component parts.

2. Review why this was a problem or challenge.

Example: This caused a 25 percent loss in revenue for the first two quarters as well as a huge buildup in back orders.

</td></tr>
</table>

3. Explain *your* role in resolving the problem or handling the challenge.

Example: I secured a secondary supplier who was able to meet the demand and deliver merchandise in half the time.

4. Describe the results achieved.

Example: As a result, the company was able to increase production by an additional 10 percent, and not only were we able to fill all existing back orders, but we also achieved record production for the third quarter.

Answering the FAQs

Be prepared to answer the proverbial abstract or unscripted questions such as, "Tell me about yourself." This open-ended inquiry is designed intentionally to see what *you* choose to talk about. The way in which you respond can be very telling about who you are, and what's important to you.

Here are some other rather common, yet fairly telling, open-ended questions that you should be prepared to answer:

Question: When I contact your previous boss, what will he or she say about you?

If you enjoyed a positive relationship with your previous boss, your answer may be that you think he or she would say you were a great employee and that he or she hated to see you leave. If the relationship was less than stellar, this is your opportunity to explain your side of the story. Not every workplace situation is perfect. Be honest, but think about your answer in advance so you won't be caught off guard.

Question: Why should we hire you over the others?

If you don't have a reason why you should be hired over other candidates, your interviewer probably won't see a reason either. Be prepared to explain the many ways in which you can contribute to the company's continued success.

Question: In what areas do you feel you need improvement?

We all have areas in which we excel, and others where there's room for growth. Respond with an answer that's honest but not too damning. For example, "When projects fall behind schedule, I can sometimes be impatient in getting things back on track."

Question: Why are you looking to move from your current position?

If you're working with a search consultant, a good answer might be that you were not looking to move, but rather were presented with an opportunity that sounded interesting and felt you would be remiss not to check it out further.

Question: What are your greatest strengths and weaknesses?

The key here is to answer with a weakness that's really a strength. For example, "In the past, I may have been a little too results-oriented. But through the years I've learned that occasionally the desired end result takes time, and you can't force the process." Of course, your strengths will come easier. Pick the top two or three that you feel relate most closely to the job and describe them in the context of the position.

Question: Why is our company appealing to you?

You've done considerable homework, so you should be very well primed to give a strong response. Impress the interviewer with a well-thought-out list of reasons, which not so coincidentally, also demonstrate your knowledge of his or her company. But don't go overboard, and don't attempt to demonstrate your astuteness by bringing up too many negatives about the company.

Here's a real-world example that illustrates how answers to these questions can ruin your chances. A colleague was conducting a search for the Executive Director of a large public service agency. When the client and the candidate met for the interview over breakfast, the candidate launched into a litany of everything that was wrong with the agency: "the board's too large, the board's too involved, the planning process is flawed, there are too many conflicting agendas at play," and so on. The client said, "If we didn't already know what our problems were, we wouldn't be here speaking with you. What we're really here for is to find out how you might be able to solve the problems."

It's one thing to make a few observations to convey that you are aware of the challenges the company faces, but it's quite another to be perceived as lecturing the interviewer.

Stuff Happens

Everyone knows that even the best employees sometimes lose their jobs. If this has happened to you, be prepared to volunteer this information so that you can communicate your side of the story and cast yourself in the most favorable light possible. Don't be bitter or accusatory. An individual who has left a company or who has been fired is still a viable candidate.

People also understand that sometimes new positions just don't work out. If that's the case, explain the situation. If the job was misrepresented, then say so. Keep in mind that if a new job doesn't go well, you shouldn't stick around for weeks or months. Once you're sure it's not a good fit, leave right away. It's far easier to explain if you leave immediately than if you end up doing so after a year or 18 months.

The Gatekeepers

Secretaries, administrative assistants, and receptionists can be very influential in the success of your candidacy. They not only determine who gets to see Mr. or Ms. Big and for how long, but their opinions also carry a fair amount of weight, especially when the perception is negative. When a candidate is unusually harried or ill-mannered, these gatekeepers make sure to pass that information along to the decision-maker. Normally they're not too bashful about voicing their impressions, and they don't mince their words. Their feedback might be something along the lines of, "Surely you're not thinking of hiring that jerk, are you?" Go out of your way to be polite and cordial to the gatekeepers. Your behavior toward potential subordinates is very telling about the kind of person you really are.

> **Secret #19**
>
> Never overlook the importance of the gatekeepers.

The book on Southwest Airlines entitled *NUTS!*, drives, or should we say, "flies" this point home. According to the book, there was a highly decorated military pilot with some of the best "on paper" credentials anyone could ever hope to have. However, on the way to the interview, the pilot was discourteous to a customer service agent and displayed a somewhat condescending attitude toward the receptionist. Of course, these are cardinal sins anywhere, but especially in the Southwest Airlines culture. The pilot may be outstanding at landing planes, but he didn't land a job with Southwest.

Spur-of-the-Moment Meetings

It's a good idea to have a brief two-minute version of your professional history rehearsed and ready-to-go. If the initial interview goes well, you may be invited on the spur-of-the-moment to meet some of the other key members of the staff. Since these meetings are unanticipated, the individuals will likely have very little time available. When they ask you about your background, you'll be prepared to recount an abbreviated rundown of the highlights of your experience. Think of this as your two-minute "Me, Incorporated" commercial. Be warm, confident, enthusiastic, and, most of all, be brief.

> **Secret #20**
>
> Have an abbreviated summary of your professional history ready to go.

Dress Rehearsal

If you have the time and access to the equipment, you may want to consider videotaping a mock interview. Compile questions you feel are likely to be asked and have a friend or colleague play the role of interviewer while the camera is rolling. Then review the tape. You'll learn a tremendous amount from it, and your interview skills will be much sharper because of this extra effort. It's better to make your mistakes during the rehearsal than after the curtain goes up.

Also, if you have several interviews scheduled, it's best to interview first with the company in which you have the least interest, and last with the company in which you have the most interest. That way, you'll be able to learn from your earlier mistakes, and you'll be much better prepared when your performance counts most.

Remain Positive

> ### Secret #21
>
> Approach each interview as though it were the best opportunity ever.

The job search process can be frustrating. It's sometimes difficult to remain positive when you've been disappointed so many times before. Try to approach each interview as a new opportunity, and prepare aggressively so you can be at your best. Treat each interview as if it's the job you've always dreamed of, at the ideal salary, in the ideal location, working for the ideal boss; even though you may have some reservations about the position going in. Your subconscious attitude will be visible to the interviewer.

Put yourself in the position of having the opportunity to reject the company's offer if you decide the job isn't right for you, rather than vice versa. There's no telling where your interview could lead if the interviewer is impressed with you. Always strive to make the best possible impression and leave all of your bridges intact.

Sleep Tight

With all your research and planning, it may be difficult to get a good night's sleep. However, it's critical that you're well rested prior to the interview. Go to bed early secure in the knowledge that you're well prepared. Two of the main attributes interviewers look for in a candidate are energy and enthusiasm. And it's hard to make a good impression after only four hours of sleep!

Secret #22

Be well rested for the interview.

Preparing for the Interview Checklist

- ❏ Do your research.
- ❏ Practice selling yourself using features and benefits.
- ❏ Anticipate abstract or unscripted questions.
- ❏ Organize your answers using the Melançon Formula.
- ❏ Be thoroughly knowledgeable about your background.
- ❏ Be courteous to the gatekeepers.
- ❏ Prepare and rehearse a two-minute "commercial" on Me, Incorporated.
- ❏ Videotape a mock interview.
- ❏ Remain positive.
- ❏ Be well rested for the interview.

Notes:

_____

_____

_____

_____

_____

_____

_____

_____

_____

CHAPTER 7

Dressing for the Interview

A Stitch in Time

FROM THE SEARCH FILES

Once, a candidate was referred to a client in California to interview for the position of Director of Strategic Planning. He wore a dark blue suit to the interview, looked impeccable, and performed extremely well all day. The very excited hiring manager called us that same afternoon and said, "You did a great job. . . . He's exactly what we've been looking for. . . . We're putting the salary offer together right now."

The hiring manager asked the candidate to stop by his office the next morning so he could share a copy of the company's strategic plan with him. Unbeknownst to the candidate, the manager also planned to introduce him to the company President and present him with an offer of employment.

Regrettably, the candidate decided to stop by on his way back to the airport and showed up wearing a pair of shorts, sandals, and a sport shirt. Not surprisingly, the hiring manager called us to say, "We just can't risk having someone represent our company who doesn't understand how to dress in a place of business." To this day the candidate still can't figure out what he "said" to turn the client off so abruptly.

The interview is never over!

Have you ever heard this before? "If you notice the person, the clothes are right. If you notice the clothes, the clothes are wrong."

In a perfect world, we would all be judged on our character and credentials alone, not on our appearance. But alas, human nature being what it is, people are judged less by what they are and more by what they *appear* to be. This is especially true in the interview setting. However, by recognizing this, you can turn it to your advantage.

The purpose of the interview is to measure and evaluate the *person*. If this weren't the case, the hiring process would culminate with the resume. One way to significantly enhance your odds for success is to make it easy for the interviewer to envision you filling the role. To accomplish this, dress for the interview as though you already hold the position you're seeking. By looking the part, the interviewer will automatically begin picturing you as part of the team, successfully interacting with clients and senior staff.

> **Secret #23**
>
> Dress for the interview as though you already hold the position.

Office Attire

You've probably noticed that there's a hierarchy when it comes to office attire. If you want to go a step further to increase your chances for success, dress like the boss or the boss' boss. How do you know what to wear? Here again, your research is key. Most companies have a reputation for dress—some for being casual, some for being ultraconservative. Make sure you know the protocol in advance and emulate the style and manner of dress prevalent in the company where you'll be interviewing. For example, the banking industry is renowned for being conservative, so a dark-colored, pinstriped suit and white shirt or blouse is always a good bet. But, if you're interviewing with a retail organization, you probably should place more emphasis on fashion and style. If you're meeting with a computer software company in Silicon Valley . . . well, anything goes!

If you are still unsure about what to wear to the interview, always err on the side of conservatism. Even companies known for a relaxed environment and casual clothing expect candidates to dress professionally for the interview. While senior management in the high-tech world may wear khaki pants and golf shirts, you shouldn't . . . at least not to the interview. Don't feel as though you must wear a tie or scarf, but do wear a stylish shirt or blouse, dress pants or a skirt, and a sport coat or jacket.

Look the part and put special emphasis on a professional appearance. You may not be as comfortable in a suit as in a knit pullover, but comfort isn't the reason you're there. The interviewer will be duly impressed with your professional attire, even in the most casual of corporate cultures. Loren Wells, Principal of Wells Reed Company, explains it this way: "I've never had a candidate rejected for dressing too conservatively, but I've had several rejected for not dressing conservatively enough!" If you're not sure about the company's style of dress, just look at the pictures in their annual report!

Here's a real-world example of how improper dress can cause your candidacy to self-destruct. We were once conducting a search for a Senior Accident Reconstruction Engineer for a prominent consulting firm in the Southwest. A would-be candidate was investigating a crash in the same city as the firm's office, and decided he would just drop by to see if he could introduce himself as a potential candidate for the position. He showed up—fresh from the crash site—wearing a sweaty shirt, dirty jeans, and muddy cowboy boots. Not only did he annoy the President of the firm immensely by dropping by unannounced, but also his appearance couldn't have been worse. The President just shook his head and said, "You just have to wonder what people are thinking sometimes!"

Face it. Fashion doesn't come naturally for everyone. We're not all subscribers to *GQ* or *Vogue*. So, if you're concerned about the appropriateness of your dress, don't hesitate to ask for professional help or consult one of the many books that are available on the subject, such as, *New Dress for Success* (Warner Books, 1988), or *New Women's Dress for Success* by John T. Molloy (Warner Books, 1996). Here's a word of caution, though. Don't let anyone advise you who isn't intimately familiar with the industry you're considering. Occasionally spouses, who know little or nothing about business attire in a specific industry, will try to dress their wives or husbands in a manner that is unsuitable (pardon the pun) for an interview. Inappropriate dress can put your candidacy in a position that's difficult, if not impossible, to overcome.

If All Goes Well

Keep in mind that, if you make a good first impression, it's likely you'll be invited back to talk further with other members of management, including the person you interviewed with initially. Have a sufficient wardrobe for at least three rounds of interviews with the same company. Don't wear the same suit or dress more than once. If you're doing a great deal of interviewing, you might even want to make a note of what you wore on each occasion to avoid a repeat performance from a clothing perspective.

Looking Your Best

Personal grooming is also very important. First impressions really do make a difference, and most firms put a great deal of emphasis on appearance.

Depending on the industry, here are a few suggestions:

▮ Your hair should be neatly styled.

▮ Men should be closely shaven.

▮ Make-up should be light and appropriate to the setting.

▮ Jewelry should be tasteful and conservative.

▮ Cologne or perfume should be very light or nonexistent.

▮ Fingernails, for both men and women, should be clean and neatly filed or manicured.

It may sound far-fetched, but at one company the entire postinterview discussion centered on a candidate's *earrings* rather than her *qualifications*. Another company ruled out a candidate based on shoes that were inappropriate for the season. Is it right? No. Is it relevant? No. Does it happen? Yes, all the time! You want to make a highly professional impression so that the focus will be on your credentials, not your grooming or wardrobe.

Dressing for the Interview Checklist

- ❏ Dress as though you already hold the position.
- ❏ Dress like senior management.
- ❏ Always err on the side of conservatism.
- ❏ Be prepared with an appropriate wardrobe for at least three rounds of interviews.
- ❏ Don't wear the same suit or dress more than once.
- ❏ If you need advice, consult a professional, or a widely accepted book on the subject of appropriate business attire.
- ❏ Don't overlook the importance of personal grooming.

Notes:

_____

_____

_____

_____

_____

_____

_____

_____

_____

_____

CHAPTER 8

The Interview

It's Showtime!

FROM THE SEARCH FILES

We once referred a candidate to a fairly sophisticated Fortune 500 client in connection with a Director of Employee and Organizational Development search we were conducting. The candidate held a Ph.D. in Industrial & Organizational Psychology, had substantial experience in both training and organizational development in the public sector, and was very well qualified for the position.

Since he had made very few job changes in his career we were careful to coach the candidate on the various do's and don'ts of the interview process, such as how to dress, how to take notes discretely, the importance of asking meaningful questions, and so on. Unfortunately, I forgot to mention that it's considered bad form to bring your dog with you to the interview—which he did!

Needless to say, the interview was a "doggone" disaster.

The interview is an art form—no two are exactly alike. As you prepare for the conversation, don't think: "What's in it for me?" Think: "What's in it for my customer? Why should he or she be interested in me?" Only about half of the jobs filled each year are those with a vacancy; the rest exist solely in the mind of the decision-maker. If sufficiently impressed, the hiring manager will create a place for you on the team. But you've got to communicate convincingly that you're the right person. And that's where the interview comes in.

Getting Started

> **Secret #24**
>
> View the decision-maker as your customer.

There's no worse feeling than running late for a really important engagement. The stress level skyrockets, palms get sweaty, and you become mentally distracted. Allow plenty of time to get to the interview. Plan your route and leave early. You'll want to arrive relaxed with sufficient time to collect your thoughts and stop by the rest room for a quick review. Is your hair neat, tie straight, slip hanging? It's natural to feel a bit apprehensive. Work on turning your nervous energy into a catalyst for peak performance.

Once you walk in the door, remember the importance of the gatekeepers. The interview process begins the moment you enter the reception area. When your interviewer comes out to greet you, offer a warm, convincing handshake. Make eye contact and be enthusiastic, but poised. As you get settled, try to relax.

Don't be afraid to show your sense of humor. Laughter helps to ease the tension. Remember that your interviewer may be a little nervous, too. We're all human.

Be professional, but be yourself. Otherwise, if you do get the job, you'll need to continue the charade the entire time you're with the company. Jeff Bezos, the billionaire founder of Amazon.com, says, "You cannot make a business case that you should be who you're not." That's advice worth remembering!

Power Questions

The more information you can identify about what's important to the decision-maker, the better you'll be able to relate how the features and benefits of your experience satisfy his or her needs. Sure, the interview is primarily for the decision-maker to assess your qualifications, but part of that process involves being proactive and asking meaningful questions. This will help you discover what carries the most weight with the interviewer, as well as demonstrate your mental alertness. In fact, many hiring managers judge the depth of candidates' business savvy by the questions they ask.

Don't assume that because of your extensive research, you know exactly what the hiring manager wants. Be prepared with a few probing questions designed to get the interviewer to reveal his or her plans and priorities. Here are a few examples:

- "If things go well next year, what will this organization look like?"

- "I couldn't help noticing in your annual report that you increased market share in the Southwest region last year. Has this momentum continued?"

■ "I noticed in *Business Week* that one of your competitors is moving from the right to the left. How will this impact your plans for growth?"

■ "Apparently the company's year-over-year profits were down in the fourth quarter. Can you tell me about the situation, and the prognosis for correcting it?"

■ "What do you see as the strengths and weaknesses of the company's current strategy?"

■ "What is most important to you?"

■ "What do you see as the biggest challenge to achieving your goals and objectives?"

These kinds of inquiries have a dual effect. They demonstrate your knowledge of the company while, at the same time, subtly eliciting information that you can use to your advantage. Don Hanratty offers a real-world example of the power of a good question:

The candidate was frustrated. He'd been there 40 minutes, and the company founder was taking phone calls, looking harried, and appeared not to be paying attention. As the candidate prepared to leave, he asked, "Sir, what is that pile of stuff on your desk?" The simple question proved to be quite effective. The founder went on to describe several important projects and his dismay about delays in getting them done. The candidate took this as a perfect opportunity to relate how he had handled very similar challenges in the past, and developed an on-the-spot position description *for his new job!*

Overlooking the Obvious

Just because it's clear to you how your experience applies in a dissimilar industry, that doesn't mean it will be obvious to the interviewer. Be prepared to translate how your background fills the interviewer's needs. Help him or her understand the relevance by translating how it will benefit the company. For example, you might make the case for why your experience in pharmaceutical sales is directly transferable to high-tech sales by explaining how your knowledge of product launches will benefit the company as it introduces new lines. Again, never *assume* interviewers will grasp this on their own, or that it goes without saying because it's on your resume.

If You Can't Say Something Positive . . .

Always speak professionally and positively about your most recent boss and employer. Address factual issues head-on, but stay away from personality conflicts. Bringing up areas of dispute will only make the interviewer begin to question your interpersonal skills. However, if you were put into a situation that was illegal or unethical, for example, these could be valid concerns to raise. But try to discuss them in a way that isn't negative. Expressing your *feelings* about a situation is more advantageous than making critical judgments. It's better to say, "I was being asked to conduct myself in a manner that *I felt* was unethical," instead of, "Company XYZ is unethical."

Stay the Course

If the hiring manager is spending too much time talking about the company or a recent fishing trip, don't hesitate to steer the dialogue back toward your relevant experience using the techniques discussed earlier in this book. You've got a limited amount of time to make the sale. If it's wasted, it's *your* loss!

Take Note

It's okay to bring a portfolio or tablet to jot down a few notes during the interview, as long as it's not too distracting. This will convey the sincerity of your interest and also help retain important information about the position or company that may otherwise be lost. This is especially helpful if you have multiple interviews, which can make it more difficult to keep track. Make a note of personal observations as well, such as the fact that the interviewer runs marathons or is an antique car enthusiast. Since your energy and attention will be focused on the interview and the interaction taking place, this type of personal information may be difficult to remember. Your notes will prove invaluable in personalizing your thank you letter, should you decide to send one.

> **Secret #25**
>
> Take notes selectively during the interview.

Just One More Thing

Following the interview, a decision will be made—yea or nay. As mentioned earlier in the book, that decision is typically ir-

revocable, despite any additional information that may be presented after the
fact. Otherwise, the interviewer would
have to admit that he or she completely
missed an important point. It's an ego
thing! Therefore, near the conclusion of

the interview, always ask how your experience fits with the requirements of the position. This is your final opportunity to
clear up any misunderstandings, and to make certain that the
hiring manager hasn't overlooked some critical aspect of your
background.

Often, interviewers are so focused on asking questions that
they may not be carefully listening to your answers. They may
be prepared to reject you for an invalid reason, or be making
the assumption that you don't have sufficient experience in a
particular area. If you ask, most interviewers will tell you, if
only in a general way, why they think you may not be right for
the job.

Here's an example: You say something along the lines of,
"I'm sure you must have interviewed several candidates for the
position by now. Tell me, how do you see my experience fit-
ting with the needs of the company?" The interviewer may respond with, "Well, your background is impressive, but we're
really hoping to find someone with more hands-on experience
in computing." This is your cue to follow with, "Actually, I'm
glad to hear you say that because although my resume focuses
primarily on my background in marketing, I also have a great
deal of experience with computers and even supervised my
company's networking effort in our 25 field offices around the
country. In fact, I would really enjoy being able to keep a
hand in that area."

It would be impossible to overemphasize how important

and effective this technique can be. If you miss this critically important opportunity, you're not likely to have another.

Take a Card

At the conclusion of the interview, be sure to pick up a business card. It will serve at least three important purposes:

1. It reinforces that you're a fellow professional and intend to stay in touch.

2. It provides the contact information you'll need to send a thank you letter, if you decide to do so.

3. It provides a convenient place to jot down a note or two during your office or plant tour following the interview.

It Ain't Over 'Til It's Over

Even when the "formal" interview is over and you're on a tour of the plant or complex, remember that you're still being evaluated. The camera is always rolling. How you conduct yourself during this phase of the interview process can be very telling. Use this as an opportunity to demonstrate how well you get along with others, or how comfortable you are on the manufacturing floor. Keep in mind that interviewers have a wide range of experience, and each one will have their own individual style. They're skilled at disarming you so they can get below the surface and find out who you *really* are.

> **Secret #27**
>
> Never let your guard down.

Don't let your guard down at any time, even in the parking lot, on the plant tour, or in the elevator. The interview is never over. You're constantly being evaluated. That's not to say that you shouldn't relax and be personable, but never stop being completely professional.

Interview Do's and Don'ts:

- Do have your two-minute commercial on "Me, Incorporated" rehearsed and ready-to-go. That way, if you're on the elevator on your way back down to the lobby, and you're introduced to the CEO or other key executive, you'll be well prepared to make the most of the brief opportunity.

- Do bring extra, unfolded copies of your resume to the interview in a leather-bound or other professional-looking portfolio. Occasionally, more than one person will be involved in the interview or you'll be introduced to other executives not on the schedule. This way, you'll be able to provide each person with a quality summary of your background for his or her reference.

- Don't ask about trivial things like vacation, office location, parking space, holidays, and the like in the initial interviews. All that is irrelevant anyway, unless and until the company has decided that they have enough interest to pursue you further. Your job is first to *sell* the company on your background. If you fail to impress them sufficiently in the initial interviews, it won't matter how many weeks of vacation they offer. You won't be working there!

- Don't bring up potential obstacles, such as special needs of children or time-off requirements, during the initial interviews. You can address these issues after the company has fallen in love with your qualifications.

■ Don't be oversensitive about providing dates regarding education or experience, and don't jump to the conclusion that it's being asked to find out how old you are. However, if the questions seem completely out of context or irrelevant to the position, you'll have to use your judgment on how best to respond. But always maintain your poise.

■ Don't bring up salary in the initial interviews. The interviewer will address compensation issues when appropriate. By bringing it up prematurely, you'll convey that you're primarily interested in the financial aspects of the job rather than the intrinsic opportunities it presents.

■ Don't ask: "Will the company pay to move my yacht and my two grand pianos?" This may be a very reasonable question, but job relocation issues should be addressed at the appropriate time, after the company has extended you an offer. Don't risk derailing the process prematurely with these kinds of petty issues.

Keep in mind that, once you've sold the hiring manager on your qualifications and he or she is convinced you're the right person for the job, there are always exceptions to policy. We'll deal more with this in the chapter on negotiating.

Making the Grade

Throughout this book, I've stressed the importance of research. However, I would be remiss not to reemphasize the value of doing your homework here as well. Sure, research is time-consuming. But that's what *sets you apart*. Most hiring managers feel there's nothing more discourteous, or inexcusable, than failing to do your homework prior to an interview. This can also cause you to be seen as having no more than a casual

> **Secret #28**
>
> Do your homework if you expect to make the grade.

interest in the company, or as lacking motivation, or as being just plain lazy. Your preparedness, or lack thereof, is taken as an indication of how you'll perform on the job.

Interview Checklist

❏ Arrive well ahead of time.
❏ Stop by the rest room to check your appearance.
❏ Be cordial to all employees.
❏ Bring your sense of humor.
❏ Jot down a few notes.
❏ Ask good questions.
❏ Steer the dialogue back to your experience when necessary.
❏ Communicate how your experience is applicable to the interviewer's needs.
❏ Speak professionally about your previous employers.
❏ Ask how your experience fits.
❏ Pick up a business card.
❏ Have your two-minute commercial on "Me, Incorporated" ready-to-go.
❏ Maintain your professionalism at all times.

Notes:

_____

_____

_____

_____

_____

_____

CHAPTER 9

Breakfast, Lunch, or Dinner Interviews

A Time for Grace, Not Grease!

FROM THE SEARCH FILES

While conducting a search for a Vice President of Logistics for a major international consumer products firm, I presented a highly qualified candidate from a "Big Three" automobile manufacturer. The company loved the candidate and was very impressed with his credentials. He was invited back for a second, then a third interview, which included dinner with the company President.

The morning after the dinner interview the client called to say that the company had no further interest in the candidate. It seems that during dinner the prospect buttered his bread and then licked the remaining butter from the butter knife! The President admonished the hiring manager, "Clearly this person doesn't have the business etiquette needed for any position with our company, much less one with such a high-profile."

It was a very brief dinner . . . and no dessert!

The breakfast, lunch, or dinner interview is much more than a free meal. If you're invited for one, understand that this is usually intended as their opportunity to assess your social skills, to determine how you might fit within the organization, and to evaluate how well you will represent the company. This is especially true if the job responsibilities include entertaining clients on behalf of the company. Proper business etiquette is extremely important. If you're not comfortable with your knowledge of the social graces, it may be a good idea to seek professional advice prior to the occasion. Of course, the same applies to your spouse as well.

The focus of the meeting should be on conveying your features and benefits to the company, not on enjoying the meal. You may even want to have something to eat *prior* to the meeting so you won't be hungry. You'll have little time to eat anyway, since you'll be doing most of the talking. Order strategically and eat gracefully. It's a good idea to eat light. Stay away from foods that are messy such as ribs or pasta. Salads, especially those with spinach, are notorious for clinging to your teeth. Dishes with gravy or sauces tend to drip excessively and can leave costly "souvenirs" on ties and silk blouses.

> **Secret #29**
>
> Breakfast, lunch, or dinner interviews are usually to assess your social skills.

What should you order? Fish is a good choice, as is grilled chicken breast. If you're not sure about what price range of entree to consider, it's wise to ask your host(s) what selection they would recommend. But remember, the breakfast, lunch, or dinner interview isn't about having a delicious meal. It's one more opportunity to convey how you can be an asset to the company.

Limited Libations

Avoid having an alcoholic drink at lunch, and order no more than one at dinner. Alcohol dulls your sharpness and overindulging may raise other questions.

General Tips:

- Never touch your food, with the exception of your bread or roll.

- Don't bite directly from the slice of bread or the roll. Break off a piece.

- Don't sop up gravy with your bread or roll.

- Spoon away from you when eating soup.

- If you leave the table, the napkin goes on the chair, not on the table.

- And, oh yes, don't lick the butter from the butter knife!

Even if you have a Ph.D., if you don't exhibit appropriate table manners and business etiquette, you'll be a perennial "also-ran" for key executive positions. And when your spouse will be joining you for the meal, be certain he or she has been properly coached as well.

Breakfast, Lunch, or Dinner Interview Checklist

❏ Consider eating a light meal beforehand so you won't be hungry.

❏ Order strategically.

❏ Be careful with alcohol.

❏ Use your best table manners.

❏ Communicate your strengths just as you would in a traditional interview setting.

Notes:

_____

_____

_____

_____

_____

_____

_____

_____

_____

_____

_____

CHAPTER 10

Follow-Up Letters

Snatching Defeat from the Jaws of Victory?

FROM THE SEARCH FILES

"Gary" was at the top of his game. At 42 years of age with 18 years of experience in marketing under his belt, he had mastered the fine art of selling himself and his ideas. Everything went perfectly during his first two rounds of interviews for Vice President of Marketing, and he was invited back by the client to join the Chief Executive Officer for dinner. The CEO was even more impressed with Gary than the other interviewers, and the job was Gary's to lose.

On the flight home following dinner with the CEO, Gary decided to dash off some quick notes thanking the interviewers for their time. Unfortunately, while his interpersonal skills were stellar, his written communication skills were not. As the CEO handed me Gary's letter he lamented," . . . and this is someone who's supposed to represent us to the marketplace? He sure had us fooled!"

Gary had always seen himself as a deal-maker. He delegated the administrative details to his subordinates, and had depended on others to do his writing for so long that his ability to compose a coherent thank you note had long since vanished. Unfortunately for Gary, so did this job opportunity!

Follow-up letters can be a double-edged sword. They can provide an excellent opportunity to seal the deal, or they can provide a perfect chance to blow everything you've done up to that point! Unfortunately, it's not unusual for a candidate to breeze through all the preceding steps, only to send a follow-up or thank you letter that looks as though a third-grader wrote it. Don't shoot yourself out of the saddle with poorly composed correspondence.

> **Secret #30**
>
> Think twice before sending a follow-up or thank you letter.

A good follow-up letter will thank the interviewer for his or her time and state how much you appreciated having the opportunity to meet. The letter should reiterate your interest in the company, and communicate how excited you are about the position.

Refer to the notes you made during the interview to help you close the letter with a personal touch. This adds a bit of humanity and demonstrates that you view the hiring manager as a person, not just as a representative of the company. For example, if the hiring manager mentioned his or her upcoming Caribbean cruise during the interview, you might write, "I hope you enjoy the beach in St. Thomas." If the two of you talked about the interviewer's interest in golf, you might add, "Have you seen the new gap wedge that TaylorMade just introduced? It sounds like just what you've been wanting for around the green."

Follow-up letters should never be more than a couple of paragraphs long and should be drafted immediately following the interview. Most experts agree that handwritten thank you notes are warmer and more personal. However, if your penmanship resembles that of a physician, it's better to type it. The same applies to the envelope.

A properly crafted follow-up letter can certainly bolster your position. Here's a real-world example of how it can work.

An executive in the insurance industry was interviewing for the position of Administrative Director. The initial screening interviews went well and he was invited back. The subsequent interviews went okay too, but the executive felt he had not sold himself and his abilities very well, nor had he adequately conveyed his enthusiasm for the job. Following his final interview, he spent an entire day writing, re-writing, and re-re-writing a follow-up letter, which featured his "90 day action plan" for attacking the key priorities of the position. The executive had done his homework, asked meaningful questions, and listened carefully during the interview, so he was well prepared—and his letter was right on target!

He was eventually offered the job, and accepted the position. Subsequently, he learned that his follow-up letter was the key in separating him from the two other finalists. The hiring manager said the executive's focus, initiative, and enthusiasm set him apart from the rest. In short, his *strategy* gave him the *advantage* over the competition and *positioned* him to win the job.

Looking Perfect in Print

All the rules that apply to cover letters also apply to follow-up letters. Be sure to double-check for typographical errors and grammatical mistakes. If you're not absolutely certain about your ability to craft an excellent letter, it's probably safer not to send one at all.

Follow-Up Letter Checklist

❏ Keep it brief.

❏ Convey warmth and enthusiasm.

❏ Communicate your interest in the company and the job.

❏ Type the letter unless you have very good penmanship.

❏ Double-check for typographical errors and grammatical mistakes.

❏ Send the letter as soon as possible following the interview.

Notes:

_____

_____

_____

_____

_____

_____

_____

_____

_____

_____

_____

_____

CHAPTER 11

Preemployment Testing

Tool or Crutch?

FROM THE SEARCH FILES

An associate was once asked to take a battery of preemployment tests by a major pharmaceutical manufacturing firm in connection with his candidacy for Director of Human Resources. Part of the process included an interview with the company's psychologist. All was well until the psychologist asked about his personal finances, to which he responded, "Frankly that's none of your business." The psychologist replied, "Well, then, I guess the interview is over." My associate followed that with, "I guess so."

As it turned out, he ended up being the top contender for the position and was told that the purpose for the questions about his personal finances was to see if he had "limits" beyond which he couldn't be pushed. He told the company representatives that while he appreciated their continued interest in him, he had no further interest in working for them.

His "limits" also included working for a company that had so little regard for an individual's privacy!

Preemployment testing is controversial. Most companies gave up the practice many years ago, primarily because it cost so much to validate the tests in order to prove they weren't discriminatory. However, they appear to be gaining popularity once again, especially for higher-level executive positions. These tests are usually designed to evaluate the candidate's personality, temperament, interpersonal skills, communication style, aptitude, and so on. Proponents of the tests say they provide an indication of how a candidate would fit within the organizational culture, and relate to the management team.

The Value of Testing

When used correctly, testing can be a valuable tool in the selection process.

According to Don Hanratty, "Testing works best when used as a piece of a larger puzzle." In his experience, most companies only give tests to finalists or other serious candidates, as well as to incumbent top-level executives; and the results aren't given all that much weight. He suggests that you "relax and use the results to your advantage."

Keith Nave agrees: "Test results should be viewed only as one part of the whole picture, including interviews, references, and the like. They should not be viewed in a vacuum." He also sees an increase in the use of testing, especially at the mid-management level. Nave cites two examples of how testing proved to be beneficial to candidates:

> Following a battery of tests, one of his clients, a tax accountant with a billion dollar electronics firm, discovered that she was totally miscast in that field. She resigned to pursue her teaching certificate and is now employed as a teacher. She's making half the money, but she's twice as happy!

In another instance, a Vice President of Engineering for a management consulting firm completed a series of tests only to confirm that she was perfectly right for her chosen profession—just in the wrong environment.

But while the tests are designed to be part of an overall assessment process, as Hanratty and Nave suggest, too often weak or untrained managers use the results as the sole selection device. We all have weaknesses or areas where we need improvement. However, professionals are well aware of their weaknesses, and work extra hard to ensure that they don't impact performance. So, rejecting a candidate solely because he or she scores poorly on some aspect of a test may actually be more indicative of a weakness in the *hiring manager* than in the candidate. Thus, preemployment tests can easily become a crutch for mediocre managers.

Another downside to testing is that it can be an *extremely expensive* proposition for the employer. The administration and scoring of the tests themselves are costly, and so are the legal fees that may be necessary to defend the company against lawsuits filed by rejected candidates—even when the company has done nothing wrong. And, if the company is found "at fault," the potential jury awards can be astronomical. It seems far more cost-effective to invest in training the company's management properly.

Evening the Score

If you're asked to take a written test, or tests, in connection with your candidacy, you'll simply have to decide just how badly you want to remain in consideration for the position.

> **Secret #31**
>
> Always ask for a copy of your test results and the interpretation.

One potential solution may be to agree to the tests, but with the assurance that you'll receive a copy of the results and the interpretation. At least that way, you'll be on equal footing with the decision-maker, and can explain anything in the report that may seem amiss. You also have the right to know who will have access to the results and for how long. If you decide to proceed with the testing, do so with a positive frame of mind or don't participate at all. Your mental attitude will affect the results.

Drug Screening

Preemployment drug screening is a different issue. It's considered a standard employment practice now, and refusing to take the test is usually not an option. So, always be prepared to submit to drug screening as a condition of employment.

Preemployment Testing Checklist

❏ Use test results for your personal growth.
❏ Ask for a copy of the test results and the interpretation.
❏ If you decide to take the tests, do so with a positive frame of mind.
❏ Be prepared for preemployment drug screening.

Notes:

_____
_____
_____
_____
_____
_____
_____
_____
_____
_____
_____
_____
_____
_____

CHAPTER 12

Salary Questions

The Moment of Truth

FROM THE SEARCH FILES

We recently conducted a search for a Director of International Compensation and Benefits on behalf of a very large petroleum exploration and production company. The candidate we presented was extremely well-qualified. The interview process went exceedingly well, and the client was prepared to make the candidate an offer when the subject of compensation arose.

The candidate was aware that the offer would include an attractive base salary, bonus, stock options, automobile allowance, and a health club membership. Unbelievably, he announced to the hiring manager that in order for him to seriously consider making a move, he would also need to be compensated for the amount of retirement income he would forfeit had he remained with his present company until retirement—nine years down the line!

We apologized to our client for the candidate's naïveté, and withdrew his name from consideration. His company subsequently announced that it was relocating to another state, and they were eliminating the candidate's position—which, of course, was why he was so anxious to find another job in the first place. He's been unemployed for a little over a year now!

This candidate should have "retired" his unrealistic expectations before they "retired" him from consideration for this position!

At some point in the interview process, the interviewer will bring up the important subject of compensation. As a professional, you should know your current compensation package to the penny, including how the base salary, performance bonus, stock options, strike price, and so on are calculated. Don't guess, and don't say you'll need to check your pay stub!

Be honest, thorough, and professional. Don't be unrealistic or misleading. Compensation means what you're *currently* earning, not what you have been promised, or what you expect to be earning in six months. And don't confuse fringe benefits with direct compensation. Company discounts, covered parking, paid holidays, and a key to the executive rest room aren't considered compensation! Suggesting otherwise will cast you in a highly unprofessional light.

> **Secret #32**
>
> Salary dialogue is like a mating dance. Get comfortable with the steps.

Playing the Numbers Game

If an interviewer asks you about your compensation requirements or expectations, it's best to be somewhat vague. If you mention a number that's too high, you may torpedo your own candidacy. If you mention a number that's too low, you risk leaving a substantial amount of money on the table.

You might handle it this way: "As I mentioned, I currently earn X. However, the scope and breadth of this position are substantially different from my current position, and I would anticipate a salary commensurate with that increased level of responsibility." Another approach might be: "I'm in the early stages of my search, and I'll be able to respond to that question more specifically after I've met with the other companies with whom I'll be interviewing."

> **Secret #33**
>
> The key to winning the "salary expectations game" is to keep the ball in the interviewer's court.

If you've already received an offer from another company, it may be smart to say so. This will demonstrate that you're taking the job search process seriously and may help to tilt the offer to the higher side. It may also enhance your attractiveness once the hiring manager sees you're in demand. Perception is important!

Don't give the specifics of the other offer; just indicate that you hope the company will put their best foot forward given your background and the responsibilities of the position. If the hiring manager makes an offer that you feel is unattractive vis-à-vis the other(s) you've received, it's okay to let them know that—*after you receive their offer.* You don't want to appear to be playing one offer against the other, and you also don't want them to scale back the offer so that it's just enough to best the competition. Offers are almost always subject to negotiation anyway.

Here are some other ideas for responding to questions about salary expectations:

- ■ "I'd be open to a competitive offer based on my experience and the scope of the position."

- ■ "I think that as you become more familiar with my background and experience, and I understand the requirements of the position more thoroughly, we'll both have a better idea about compensation. Knowing the reputation of your company, I'm sure it will be a fair offer."

Without appearing evasive, try to keep the onus on the hiring manager to be the first to suggest a salary offer or package. If you're working with a search consultant, he or she can be extremely beneficial in coaching you through this process and negotiating with the employer on your behalf without allowing things to become confrontational.

Beyond Dollars

Be sure to convey that you're primarily interested in the challenges of the position, and that while compensation is important, it's a secondary consideration. Putting too much emphasis on money, as opposed to the opportunity, is a mistake. Communicate how impressed you are with the company, and how excited you are about the challenge that the position represents. Explain that you'll be evaluating the whole package, not just the dollars. If appropriate, mention that other aspects of compensation are also important including stock participation, equity interest, and so on.

If relocation is involved, you may want to let the hiring manager know what you would be forfeiting in terms of your spouse's compensation. Don't expect the employer to cover this, of course, but it may be helpful to make them aware that this will be a factor you'll have to consider as you weigh your options. It can often result in a more generous offer than might otherwise have been made.

Salary Gymnastics

Generally speaking, it's smart to be flexible in salary expectations. But being too flexible can actually *hurt* your chances. For example, if you earned $120,000 in your previous position but would now be willing to consider an opportunity paying $75,000, most hiring managers would assume that there's a problem somewhere. Again, perception is key.

> **Secret #34**
>
> Being too flexible can depreciate your candidacy.

Salary Questions Checklist

❏ Be honest about your current compensation.
❏ Know exactly how all facets of your compensation are calculated.
❏ Don't reveal the details of other offers.
❏ Be vague about your compensation expectations.
❏ Be flexible regarding salary, but not too flexible.

Notes:

_____

_____

_____

_____

_____

_____

_____

_____

_____

_____

_____

_____

_____

CHAPTER 13

The Offer

Negotiating for Pennies

FROM THE SEARCH FILES

We were engaged in an assignment for a major aerospace and defense contractor, and we presented a candidate for Vice President of Procurement. While this particular candidate was certainly qualified for the position, he didn't have as strong a background as some of the others under consideration. That's why we were a bit surprised when he wound up as the top prospect, and was presented with a very attractive offer including a base salary, which represented a significant increase, plus bonus, stock, car, and full relocation including home purchase.

We thought the candidate would be doing back flips over the offer, but instead he calmly indicated that, while it sounded attractive, he wished to meet with the hiring manager again to discuss the package further. We were concerned that he was going to muddy the waters and miss out on a great opportunity. But the protracted negotiations went off without a hitch and the candidate wound up improving the offer in several areas.

When the subject came up several weeks later, the hiring manager told me that he would have been extremely disappointed if the candidate had not *pressed for a better offer. "If he's not effective negotiating on his own behalf, how's he going to be effective negotiating on the company's behalf?"*

When it comes to the job offer, Dr. Chester Karrass is right, "In business, you don't get what you deserve, you get what you negotiate."

When considering a career move, it's often difficult to gauge just what might be appropriate in terms of compensation. What's important to one individual may be relatively unimportant to another. So, the "right" package can vary greatly from person to person. This is where your career/life planning efforts will be extremely helpful.

In a perfect world, the overall accountability or responsibility of the position would be used to determine the salary offer. If you're able to handle the job, then you should be paid what the job is worth—without regard to your current compensation. In the real world, however, it doesn't work that way. Salary offers are almost always computed as a percentage increase above the candidate's present salary. As a rule of thumb, a 10 to 20 percent increase is fairly typical if the position doesn't require relocation, and 20 percent or more is prevalent if it does. Of course, it all depends on how much they want you, and that depends on how you've done selling yourself!

You may have noticed that hiring managers and search consultants usually refrain from giving a specific dollar amount that the company may be prepared to pay. That's because the number really represents what they *might* be willing to pay for the *ideal* candidate with the *ideal* qualifications. Frequently, the successful candidate is *acceptable*, but not necessarily ideal. However, once a candidate hears a number it becomes an expectation, and anything less is viewed as a personal affront. Thus, hiring managers and search consultants usually express compensation in terms of a *range* for the position.

When evaluating an opportunity, you'll want to give careful consideration to the *entire package*. Occasionally, the base salary offered may be lower than you'd like, but that may be more than made up for in incentives, performance bonuses, or stock participation. Other components of compensation worthy of consideration might include profit sharing, stock appreciation rights/phantom stock, deferred compensation, retirement/401K programs, relocation/home purchase assistance, car or car allowance, personal time off, employee assistance programs (EAP), and the like. According to the *Harvard Business Review*, stock options have become the fastest growing segment of executive pay, and now account for more than half of total CEO compensation and 30 percent of senior operating managers' pay.

When evaluating an opportunity, be sure to consider noncompensation issues as well. Ask yourself the following:

- Will I like the work?

- Do I have a reasonable chance for success?

- Does it represent a logical, positive career move?

- Will I like the corporate culture?

- Why is the position open?

∎ Is upper-management competent?

∎ Does the company have a record of growth?

∎ Is the industry viable?

∎ Are the medical benefits sufficient?

∎ Is the location acceptable?

Your answers to these questions should weigh heavily in your decision and, for some people, may even be more significant than the direct compensation. Don't forget the MDV equation—and the relative importance of each variable.

> **Secret #35**
>
> Make your employment decision based on the opportunity, not personalities.

One thing I always warn candidates to guard against is the tendency to allow their decision-making process to be overly influenced by the personality of the person to whom they will initially be reporting. The reality is that if you're a strong performer, or your boss is a strong performer, then one of you will be moving to a new assignment quickly anyway. Make your decision based on the whole package, not the personality of one or two individuals.

Pace Yourself

When presented with an offer, never accept it on the spot. You don't want to appear to be desperate or overanxious. Be positive and appreciative. Indicate that you're flattered that the company has an interest in having you join the team. Tell the decision-maker that you want to discuss it with your spouse, if appropriate, and that you will give the offer serious consideration. Let the employer know when to expect your decision. Overnight or a couple of days is fine. But don't take longer than a week or draw the process out unnecessarily. Otherwise, it will raise questions as to your decisiveness and the sincerity of your interest.

It's not unknown for offers to be withdrawn based on the hiring manager's perception of a candidate's lack of enthusiasm. So, be careful not to give the impression that you're accepting his or her offer grudgingly or as a last resort. View the offer as an important opportunity to begin solidifying your relationship with your new boss.

Silence Can Be GOLDen

Silence can be a wonderful negotiating tool. When a company extends an offer, don't feel compelled to fill the air with words immediately. Silence gives the hiring manager an opportunity to put something else on the table if he or she is so inclined. Be confident. The offer's already in your pocket. Seldom is the first offer the best offer. Here's a real-world example of how silence can work in your favor.

> **Secret #36**
>
> In salary negotiations, he who speaks first often loses.

The interviews had gone well and the candidate had returned for a final meeting with the President and the Vice President of Marketing, at which time they presented an offer. The candidate asked if anything could be done to improve the base salary or bonus eligibility. The President indicated that the company might be able to offer $5,000 more on the base, and the Vice President chimed-in that she would see if they could make the bonus effective in six months instead of a year. The candidate said, "I really appreciate that. What else might be done?"

The President and the Vice President looked at one another and said, "We're really not sure." The candidate patiently enjoyed a few moments of silence (which seemed like an eternity). When the silence became too uncomfortable, the President said, "We'd really love to have you on our team. How about we throw in a signing bonus of $10,000." In reality, the candidate was ready to accept the offer before the initial $5,000 increase in his base. He was just putting silence to work on his behalf.

Losing the Luster

At the time the company extends the offer, there's a real glow to your candidacy. You're excited—there's nothing like feeling wanted, and the decision-maker is excited—he or she can clearly see how you will benefit the company. However, the more you haggle back and forth with the hiring manager about salary, and the longer it takes between the offer and acceptance, the more the hiring manager begins to question his or her decision. The glow begins to fade.

> **Secret #37**
>
> Negotiating for pennies can cost you a bundle.

Here's a likely scenario. A candidate is offered a base salary of $90,000. She responds with, "I'm really interested in the position, but $95,000 is more like what I had in mind." That puts the hiring manager in the position of having to go back through the approval process with his manager, his manager's manager, and Human Resources. Keep in mind that at the $95,000 level there may well be other, potentially better-qualified prospects to consider. And the difference in a few thousand dollars a year, divided by 12 months, after taxes, is negligible in your paycheck anyway. So, is such a small dollar amount really worth the risk of casting a pall over your candidacy? Think hard before negotiating for pennies.

However, if negotiating is the nature of your job as is the case in sales, purchasing/procurement, or labor relations, then haggling over any and all aspects of your offer package isn't only acceptable, it's expected! Also, for reasons I will explain in Chapter 16, negotiating for extended temporary housing allowance can be very important when the new position requires relocation. So *do* try to negotiate this in whenever possible.

Offer Checklist

❏ Consider both compensation and noncompensation factors.

❏ Take time to consider the offer; don't accept on-the-spot.

❏ Negotiate only when appropriate.

❏ Use silence to your advantage.

❏ Be careful when negotiating for pennies.

Notes:

_____

_____

_____

_____

_____

_____

_____

_____

_____

_____

_____

_____

CHAPTER 14

Offer Letters

Don't Leave Home Without One

FROM THE SEARCH FILES

"Fred" had 18 years of experience and was a Director of Manufacturing Operations when he was presented as a candidate for Vice President–Manufacturing with a major semiconductor company. Things went exceptionally well throughout the interview process. After interviewing with the President, the search consultant was instructed to proceed with the verbal offer on the company's behalf.

Upon hearing the news, the candidate commented that the timing was perfect and that he planned to tender his resignation immediately to provide maximum notice to his current employer. The consultant advised Fred not to resign until he received the company's written offer, which would be coming by FedEx.

At 2:00 P.M. the next day, the President—the person to whom Fred would report—was unexpectedly called before the board and fired! When contacted by the consultant, the new President said, "I always bring in my own team, and I already know exactly whom I want for that job."

Had Fred not taken the consultant's advice and resigned prematurely, he would have been "homeless." And, even if his old company allowed him to stay, his career there would have been a "finished product!"

If you're a top executive, and another company is trying to lure you away, you should not hesitate to ask for a written employment contract. In that case, make absolutely certain that it's either prepared, or at least reviewed, by a competent labor attorney.

However, if you're the one doing the initiating, an employment contract is probably not in the cards. In most cases, employers are reluctant to grant such contracts because of the potential they hold for working *against* the company. For example, in some contracts, all an employee might have to do is *show up* in order to satisfy the terms of the contract, and the employer would be obligated to sign the paycheck.

Secret #38

Get the offer in writing before tendering your resignation.

Nevertheless, you should *always* insist upon written confirmation of the relevant terms and conditions of your offer before giving notice to your current employer. This letter may be the most important document in your file, as well as in your pocket! Never leave your present job without a contract, offer letter, or other written confirmation of the details of the offer.

It's not the least bit unusual to see people resign on the basis of a verbal offer alone, only to find that the written offer falls far short of the terms discussed during the interview. "Candidates are notorious for hearing what they want to hear during the interview process," according to hiring managers. "Managers are notorious for reneging on their promises," according to candidates. *Get it in writing!*

If you were told that you'd be eligible for a bonus in six months, make sure it's in the offer letter. If your manager agreed to pay for your attendance at the trade association's fall conference, the letter should state that. If you were promised a position on the company's strategic task force, include that information as well. Your written offer letter may be the only protection you have if and when there's a change in your immediate management.

If you receive an offer letter and the terms and conditions are either different from what you understood or exclude important items, be sure to clarify them in writing. This can be handled in a positive way by sending a written response to the hiring manager simply clarifying your understanding. Only after the company responds to your letter of clarification with satisfactory written confirmation should you feel comfortable resigning from your present position.

In the rare case that the prospective company doesn't wish to provide an offer in writing, you should feel free to initiate your own letter of understanding and send it to the hiring manager for confirmation. Or, better yet, look elsewhere! There's probably a reason why they don't want to commit to you in writing.

Play Me Or Pay Me

> **Secret #39**
>
> Negotiate advance notice of termination or compensation in lieu of notice.

Many offer letters contain a clause stating that an individual can be fired at any time, for any reason. That's not uncommon, especially in "employment at will" states. In fact, it probably says the same thing on the company's employment application that you likely signed at some point during the process. But depending on the level of the position you're considering, it can be an excellent idea to have your offer letter state that, "The company will give you X number of weeks/months advance notice of termination of employment or change-in-control, or compensation in lieu of such notice." This isn't as formal as a contract, and may therefore be more palatable to the prospective employer. But it's *perpetually renewing*, and can provide a great deal of protection for the employee.

Offer Letters Checklist

- ❏ Secure the terms of your employment offer in writing.
- ❏ Make sure the offer letter reflects all relevant areas of discussion.
- ❏ Request written confirmation of any items not included in the original offer letter.
- ❏ Never resign from your current position until the written understanding is satisfactorily completed.
- ❏ Create your own letter of understanding when necessary.
- ❏ Negotiate advance notice of termination/change-in-control, or compensation in lieu of notice.

Notes:

_____

_____

_____

_____

_____

_____

_____

_____

_____

_____

CHAPTER 15

Counteroffers

Professional Suicide?

FROM THE SEARCH FILES

A close friend and former Director of Staffing for a major consumer products company confides:

> *It's pretty much standard practice to make a counteroffer to anyone at the mid-management-level and above who resigns. But the primary reason for doing so isn't because the company wants to keep the employee. It's only to buy some time to find a replacement! It doesn't matter how much money you promise either, because the employee will be history as soon as a replacement can be found. Once that replacement is identified, either the company will let the tainted executive go, or will make it so uncomfortable that he or she will quit. When an employee crosses the line, there's no going back either. The individual's loyalty is forever in question.*

The unfortunate reality is that, as soon as a company presents a counteroffer, the executive is in a no-win situation. If he or she declines the counteroffer and leaves, management says, "Good riddance. We don't need people who aren't loyal to the company." And, if *he or she accepts the counteroffer, management says, "See, money was all that mattered. Greedy bastard."*

Accepting counteroffers can be hazardous to your wealth!

It's sometimes uncomfortable breaking the news to your employer that you've accepted a position with another company. This is especially true if you've been with the same employer for a long time, or if it's the only job you've ever had. Once you tender your resignation you may begin feeling like a "man without a country." You're no longer considered part of the old team, and you're not yet part of the new team. You may even begin to have feelings of guilt for leaving. Your manager knows this, and will likely seize the opportunity and make a counteroffer.

Here's a scenario: You inform your boss of your decision to accept a new position with a different company. Your boss' first reaction is to question whether this is a ploy to get a pay increase or better assignment. She grudgingly accepts your resignation and says something along the lines of, "I'm really disappointed. I had just put you in for an increase, and you're next on the list for a promotion. If I can get that process sped up, will you consider staying?" You say you're not sure, but you're willing to consider it. After a few days your boss calls you into her office and says, "I've cleared it with Mr./Ms. Big, and we're prepared to accelerate your increase if you'll stay." Defaulting to your comfort zone, you agree to remain with the company.

You'll get that increase, and it will likely be a good one.

That's easy to do because they'll simply lengthen the interval between future increases. Within a couple of years, you'll be no better off than had you not accepted the counteroffer, but the company has avoided the cost of recruiting and training someone to replace you.

> **Secret #40**
>
> Accepting a counteroffer can mean a slow death for your career.

Joining the "B" Team

Once you've accepted a counteroffer, your loyalty to the company will forever be in question. When your name comes up for promotion, Mr./Ms. Big will say, "Isn't that the employee who threatened to leave awhile back? How can we reward that kind of disloyalty? We need to make this person an example!" It won't be obvious, but your career will be placed on hold. When annual pay raises come around, you'll get a smaller share of the pie. It's also likely that your coworkers will begin to feel resentment. Your career will die a slow death.

While it may be appealing in terms of short-term security or the desire to remain in a familiar environment, accepting a counteroffer is a high-risk proposition. If you're considering accepting a new position, make your decision and stick with it. When you tender your resignation, you should be ready to leave. On the other hand, if your goal is to force a salary increase or change in assignment, ask for it up front. Don't use another company's offer as a ploy. That's professional suicide. It almost always works against you in the long run, especially if you're a senior-level executive.

Loren Wells reports that in his 25-plus years in the staffing business, he has never seen a counteroffer work to an individual's advantage. In fact, "80 percent of the time the employee is gone within a year, and most often it's not by the individual's own initiation!" If you do accept a counteroffer, he strongly advises that you get a contract, "because you'll no longer be part of the 'A' team."

Accepting a counteroffer can hurt in other ways as well. By the time the new company extends an offer to you, both the hiring company and the search consultant, if involved, have a considerable amount of time, effort, and money invested in your candidacy. It's only logical that they'll want to ensure that other firms, and/or consultants, don't have the same experience working with you.

Counteroffers Checklist

❏ Counteroffers almost always have negative consequences in the long run.
❏ Evaluate the entire situation carefully.
❏ Make your decision and stick by it.

Notes:

_____
_____
_____
_____
_____
_____
_____
_____
_____
_____
_____
_____
_____
_____
_____
_____

CHAPTER 16

Ensuring Your Success

Pick the Low-Hanging Fruit

FROM THE SEARCH FILES

"Bill" was a sharp young Electrical Engineer with a master's degree from a prestigious university. He had interned with a major aerospace and defense corporation during his junior and senior years and accepted a position with a very large, well-known electronics firm upon graduation. The firm's culture was very aggressive. Senior management would vigorously challenge the work of the young engineers to ensure that they were technically accurate and constantly on their toes.

After several years, Bill accepted a position as an Engineering Manager for a smaller firm in the same industry. On the first day, *he aggressively challenged the design work of one of the physicists on staff—which was the standard approach at his previous firm. The Physicist was furious that "the new guy" would dare challenge him, and a heated argument quickly ensued.*

Some time later, Bill learned that the Physicist really had done a very good job, considering the information he had at the time. He also discovered that the company President had personally recruited the Physicist to the firm, and that they were personal friends! Bill now admits that all he accomplished was making an enemy of someone who should have been an ally, and who could have really helped him along in his career.

Bill spent the balance of his time with the new company mending fences, and trying to recover from the bad start he had inadvertently "engineered."

When starting a new job, that old axiom, "You never get a second chance to make a good first impression," may seem trite, but it's true. It's virtually impossible to recover from a bad start on the job. Everyone's perception of you, accurate or not, is set within the first few weeks. Spend that time getting a clear understanding of the expectations for the position, and then strive to exceed those expectations.

Find out what you need to do to be successful, and then do it. Arrive at work early and stay late. Seek out opportunities to be of assistance to others. Volunteer for additional responsibilities whenever appropriate.

Dangerous Distractions

Secret #41

Negotiate extended temporary housing allowance.

In the early going, it's critical that you're able to concentrate as much as possible on your new responsibilities. So, if you're required to relocate for the new position, try to negotiate extended temporary housing allowance as part of your offer package. That way you won't have to worry about selling a house, buying a new house, packing, unpacking, moving your family, and so on, at the same time you're trying to make a positive impact on the job.

The Disappearing Decision-Maker

Hiring managers look for validation. They want to know as soon as possible, "Did I hire the right person?" Their reputations are tied to the new hire's success. If the new employee performs well, they look good, and they'll be committed to making the individual look even better. But if he doesn't measure up, hiring managers will quickly distance themselves from the employee. If he isn't going to make it, hiring managers want it to be clear that it's because of the new hire's poor performance, not because they made a bad hiring decision.

A Game-Winning Strategy

People who fail in a new assignment usually do so because they take on too much, too soon. They try to hit a home run as soon as they get on the field without realizing that hitting consistent singles—with no errors—is a much safer way to win the game. Get comfortable with the playing field first, and you'll not only be more likely to put runs on the scoreboard, but you'll also be less likely to get tossed out of the game.

Secret #42

Your earliest battles should be those that are easiest to win.

Take on the challenges that are noninflammatory, or where everyone comes out a winner. Go for the low-hanging fruit. Fight the small battles first, and don't latch onto the biggest, thorniest problems right away. There's usually a reason why no one has tackled these issues before now. Don't risk alienating key executives whose support you'll need later. Get to know the political terrain and concentrate on forging alliances.

Ensuring Your Success Checklist

❏ Negotiate extended temporary housing allowance, if necessary.

❏ Focus on your new responsibilities, and eliminate distractions.

❏ Help validate the hiring manager's decision.

❏ Tackle the easiest problems first.

Notes:

_____

_____

_____

_____

_____

_____

_____

_____

_____

_____

_____

_____

_____

Personal Marketing 101

Have you ever heard it said, "The easiest way to get a loan is to prove you don't need one?" Well, a similar truism applies to the job search process. "The easiest way to find a new job is to not have to look for one." How do you accomplish this? Simply, have the job find you! Begin thinking like a hiring manager or search consultant, and make yourself easy to find.

Most successful and talented people are so completely focused on their jobs that they seldom take time to *market* themselves the way they should. After all, why bother? They're happy, challenged, and extremely busy, so another opportunity is the farthest thing from their minds. But while their work ethic may be admirable, their lack of personal marketing skills is not. Marketing "Me, Incorporated" is a continuous process and you should be constantly aware of opportunities that lead you closer to your long-term career/life goals.

Up Antenna!

When opportunity knocks, listen! You always want to be in the position of *knowing* about other opportunities, whether you have an immediate interest in them or not. It keeps you abreast of the marketplace, broadens your network, and is helpful as a measure of how your own career is progressing.

One of the basic tenets of investing is that the absolute best time to decide when you will sell an investment is *before* you buy it. If you wait until afterwards, you become too influenced by emotions to make a truly objective decision. The same is true of your career. The absolute best time to consider other opportunities is when you're happy, successful, and gainfully employed. That way you can be totally objective about the potential the new opportunity may offer, and you're in the best possible position should you decide to pur-

> **Secret #43**
>
> The best time to consider other opportunities is when you're happy where you are.

sue it. Suddenly, you're a buyer instead of a seller, and it makes a world of difference in how you're perceived throughout the process.

So, how do you put yourself in a position to *hear* about opportunities? Raise your profile! How do you get *discovered* by search consultants and hiring managers? Raise your profile!

Is your Rolodex looking a little thin? If so, you may want to increase your participation in professional associations and attendance at professional conferences and seminars. This can be an excellent way to meet new contacts, make lasting friendships, and stay on the forefront of your field.

Search consultants know how important professional associations are and use their membership rosters extensively to identify the industry's best. Active involvement in these associations, especially in a leadership position on the board, ensures that you'll be among the first to know about the very best opportunities in your field.

If you've just accepted a new position, write a short thank you note to people who may have been helpful during your search. For one thing, it's a matter of professional courtesy. For another, it's a highly appropriate opportunity to subtly let them know how well your career is advancing. And finally, it makes them aware of how to reach you should an even better opportunity arise. It can play an important first (next) step in your new and ongoing networking campaign.

Benevolent associations can be another good way to network. City and country clubs, women's organizations, and community groups also offer opportunities to raise your profile and make contact with key decision-makers. Don't underestimate the benefit of well-timed notes to fellow members. Stay in touch with friends and business associates on a regular basis. Keith Nave puts it this way, "Success in networking stems not from whom you know, but from who knows you!"

You just never know where that once-in-a-lifetime opportunity will come from. According to a recent study by Drake Beam Morin, networking is responsible for 61 percent of new hires. So, it would be hard to overstate its importance in your long-term career strategy. Here's an example of a real-world networking success story.

A partner in a major financial consulting firm had become increasingly unhappy in her job and had begun a fairly aggressive campaign to find a new opportunity. She had taken all the career tests, read all the books, written all the letters, but had met with limited success.

At a neighborhood barbecue one weekend she mentioned to a neighbor that she was interested in pursuing a new career opportunity. The neighbor's friend overheard her and suggested that she would be perfect for a position he had heard about at a recent Rotary Club meeting. The position was with "some type of medical-related firm," and hardly seemed to be a good a fit with her background. But having nothing to lose, she decided to look into it anyway.

A few weeks later she was the Administrative Manager of a high-growth medical practice management firm reporting to the Chief Executive Officer, and she is extremely happy in the position.

Some Expert Advice

> **Secret #44**
>
> Establish yourself as an industry expert.

Submitting articles and guest editorials to trade publications and business journals can help you position yourself as an expert or leader in your field. This takes time, but the benefits can be tremendous. Your current boss will be pleased to see your name in print too, since a well-written article about the industry can be a positive reflection on your company. Other leaders in the industry will take notice as well.

Public speaking engagements can be another good way to raise your professional profile. Many companies and associations have speaker's bureaus. Become involved with them and you'll see how one successful engagement leads to another, and another, and another.

Digging Wells

Author Harvey Mackay writes of the importance of digging your well before you're thirsty. In the context of employment, this takes on added significance. In an article featured in *Success* magazine, he explains, "One reason you build a network is the same reason people built bomb shelters: because someone's planning to drop the Big One on you—except this time it's called *downsizing, restructuring, or right-sizing.*"

The Latest Edition

Keep a record of your achievements, tuck away samples of your work, and update your general resume from time to time so it will reflect your new accomplishments. That way, if an unexpected opportunity comes along, you'll be ready to present your credentials without delay.

Relationships Worth Having

Search consultants are professionals, and, for the most part, are good at what they do. They're "in the know," and can be of great assistance, both directly and indirectly, throughout your career. Obviously, if you're a viable candidate for a search they're representing, they'll be able to help you *directly* by coaching you through everything from the resume, to the cover letter, to the interview, to the follow-up letter, to the negotiations, to those critical first few weeks on the job. But don't overlook the fact that these consultants can be extremely helpful *indirectly* as well.

> **Secret #45**
>
> Develop ongoing relationships with search consultants.

They're typically aware of many more opportunities than are ever made public. In fact, according to a recent study by

Coopers & Lybrand, 64 percent of executive positions are filled through executive recruiters. And, if you've developed the proper *relationship*, they can make sure that your name is introduced as a candidate for such opportunities, even though they may not be conducting the search themselves. Or, they may know the person who just left the job you're considering, and can either put in a good word on your behalf or keep you from making a big mistake. It's only good business for them to see you advance in your career—that's where their future business comes from! Following are a few tips that may be helpful in developing relationships with search consultants.

- Realize that your resume may be one of a hundred or more received by the search firm that day. If they're not working on an assignment for which you can be considered at that moment, your resume will not likely be retained (unless you have a unique background or skill).

- Be realistic in your expectations. Search consultants are paid by the client company and, therefore, must focus primarily on the client's needs, not yours. Don't call expecting them to drop everything to meet with you, especially if your background isn't in line with their current requirements. Instead, suggest lunch or a cocktail at some point down the road and work toward developing an *ongoing* relationship.

- Remember that relationships are built over time. When you receive a call from a search consultant, it's a good idea to be courteous and helpful if you can. You may not be interested in the position he is currently representing, but you may want to be considered for other opportunities down the line. Make no mistake, the "headhunter" will make a record of the call as well as how you handled yourself, and will likely share that information with other industry consultants. If you're polite and ask intelligent questions, you'll likely hear from that firm, or similar firms, again with other opportunities, which may be

> **Secret #46**
>
> Be courteous to the headhunter. The next head hunted may be your own!

more appealing. It's always better to be aware of opportunities and elect not to pursue them, than never to hear about them in the first place.

■ Don't call only when you're in trouble. Consultants find it extremely annoying to hear from executives only every few years—when they're in trouble or have lost their jobs. Contact them on a friendly basis from time to time, just to stay in touch. If you expect them to put you at the top of their list, put them at the top of yours!

■ Be particularly sensitive to developing an ongoing business relationship with the consultants who will be in the best position to help you in return. For example, if you've been placing all of your search activity with firm X, don't expect firm Y to come to your rescue at your time of need.

■ Take the time to build relationships with search consultants while you're still employed. If you're not getting at least one call a month from a search firm, then your profile is probably not high enough. If you've not heard from a search firm in three months, you've got some serious work to do.

The Career Check-Up

It's amazing what we add to our calendars—meetings, vacations, kids' activities, doctor visits, hair appointments, car maintenance, and so forth. Why not add a regular *career check-up* to that list? Unfortunately, very few professionals do this. But it's a common practice among the highly successful.

Don Hanratty advocates reviewing the success of "Me, Incorporated" on a quarterly basis: "Sit down with your employer (the customer of "Me, Incorporated") and say, 'Here's what I think we accomplished this quarter. What do you think we should be working on next quarter?' "

He also encourages his clients who may be considering a career change to visit people who are successful in their careers and learn from them. See what a day-in-the-life really is like within a field that interests you. You may find that it's very different than you imagined.

Building a successful track record and enjoying a fulfilling career doesn't just happen. *You* are responsible for your future. Continually update and refer to your career/life plan to stay on course.

In Conclusion

I hope you've enjoyed this insider's look at the secrets of executive search. These secrets can mean the difference between happiness and disappointment, satisfaction and frustration, success and failure in your quest for the *right* career opportunity. They work, and I encourage you to use them to your advantage!

The personal search process is not easy, and like the great

chess masters, you must be prepared to invest a considerable amount of time, effort, and self-discipline to develop the skills necessary for success. It will likely be the most important investment you will ever make. And, like any other worthwhile endeavor, the more you put in to it, the more you can expect to get out of it!

Proceed with confidence. You now have the knowledge, tools, and techniques necessary to be the "master" of your career. It's your move!

> I prepare myself well. I know what I can do before I go in. I'm always confident.
>
> —Robert J. "Bobby" Fischer,
> World Chess Champion, 1972

Notes:

Industry Overview

Employment agencies, headhunters, executive recruiters, search consultants—those in the employment industry go by many names. But while they share some similarities, in fact they're vastly different in terms of how they function, and how they are compensated for their efforts. This appendix offers a brief description of the advantages and disadvantages of each.

Employment or Personnel Agencies

Employment or personnel agencies are in the business of *assisting the individual* with finding a job. These companies may help with resume preparation, offer minimal job search advice, and arrange "send-outs" for the candidate to interview with prospective employers. In return for this assistance, the *candidate* is typically responsible for the agency's fee—regardless of whether the candidate is successful in finding employment. This type of service is most often used for filling entry-level or nonprofessional positions.

Contingency Firms

Contingency, or placement firms, also assist *individuals* seeking employment, typically sending out numerous copies of a candidate's resume to companies they hope may have an interest. Since their employment fee is *contingent* upon someone actually hiring the individual, their primary incentive is to send your resume to as many companies as possible—something of a numbers game. Therein lies the potential downside. Basically the candidate has no control over where their resume may show up. But if this isn't a concern, then contingency firms could be a viable way to get your resume in front of a host of potential employers.

Retainer-Based Executive Search Firms

True retainer-based executive search firms operate on a contractual basis and *assist the company* in identifying candidates for a specific position. In other words, they represent a position seeking a person rather than a person seeking a position. Thus, the term *headhunter*. Since most candidates identified are not actively looking for a new position at the time, the search consultant's goal is to fill the position to the mutual satisfaction of both the hiring company and the candidate. Because the executive search process is considerably involved and time-consuming, the client company is obligated to pay the consultant for his time—regardless of whether anyone is ultimately hired. Traditionally, retainer-based executive search firms represent senior-level opportunities.

Since the search consultant's fee is guaranteed, he or she can afford to invest the time and effort necessary to make certain that the candidate is fully qualified and the *best prospect available* for the client's position. In addition, the search consultant will be in a better position to ensure that the opportunity is also an appropriate career move for the candidate, given the candidate's career goals and aspirations.

Usually, retainer-based executive search firms are far more forthcoming and open with information. They'll generally tell you up front who the client is, and are able to share an abundance of information about the position. A possible downside of working with these firms is that they will only consider you for one job at a time, with one client at a time. However, you can be sure that they will consider you *only* for the position discussed, and your resume will not leave their office without your approval. In addition, they'll quickly let you know if you don't have the necessary qualifications, so you'll always know where you stand.

The upside is that search consultants represent many of the *hidden jobs* that are often filled before anyone even knows they're available. Also, search consultants can pave the way for your success by ensuring that your candidacy is positioned in the best manner possible.

Should you receive a call from a recruiter, it may be helpful to ask a few simple questions to qualify the caller as the lines between search, contingency, and placement are sometimes blurred. Retainer-based executive search consultants will appreciate that you're qualifying them, so they can qualify you in return. Ask the consultant on what basis he is engaged in the assignment, and request his name and phone number for future reference.

A retainer-based executive search consultant will almost always be able to answer the following questions with ease.

- What is the organizational structure of the company?

- What are the reporting relationships above and beneath this position?

- What is the budget or staff for which this position is responsible?

- Why is the position open?

- Have you met the hiring manager? What is his or her background?

- How is the position compensated?

- Can the consultant provide you with a 10-K, proxy statement, annual report, and so on?

Only after you're confident that you're speaking with a true retainer-based executive search consultant should you feel comfortable providing personal information about yourself and your experience. Otherwise, you may find your resume under windshield wipers at the local shopping center!

Notes:

_____

_____

_____

_____

_____

_____

_____

_____

_____

_____

_____

_____

_____

_____

_____

_____

_____

_____

_____

_____

_____

_____

The Secrets

Secret #1:   Beware of the activity trap.

Secret #2:   Approach your search in reverse.

Secret #3:   Position yourself as a problem-solver.

Secret #4:   Customize each resume to the requirements of the position sought.

Secret #5:   Never underestimate the importance of a well-written resume.

Secret #6:   Orient your resume to the reader.

Secret #7:   Make sure you're perfect in print.

Secret #8:   Include a keyword summary in your hard copy resume.

Secret #9:   Promote yourself with the cover letter.

Secret #10: Make contact two or three levels above the position sought.

Secret #11: Appeal to the decision-maker's self-interest.

Secret #12: Knowing the "code" will give you the advantage.

Secret #13: Install a dedicated second phone line with voice mail.

Secret #14:   Be sure you know what your references will say.

Secret #15:   "Close the loop" with your references.

Secret #16:   Use features and benefits to make the sale.

Secret #17:   Be intimately familiar with all aspects of your background.

Secret #18:   Use Melançon's Formula to provide a thorough response.

Secret #19:   Never overlook the importance of the gatekeepers.

Secret #20:   Have an abbreviated summary of your professional history ready to go.

Secret #21:   Approach each interview as though it were the best opportunity ever.

Secret #22:   Be well rested for the interview.

Secret #23:   Dress for the interview as though you already hold the position.

Secret #24:   View the decision-maker as your customer.

Secret #25:   Take notes selectively during the interview.

Secret #26:   Always ask how you fit.

Secret #27:   Never let your guard down.

Secret #28:   Do your homework if you expect to make the grade.

Secret #29: Breakfast, lunch, or dinner interviews are usually to assess your social skills.

Secret #30: Think twice before sending a follow-up or thank you letter.

Secret #31: Always ask for a copy of your test results and the interpretation.

Secret #32: Salary dialogue is like a mating dance. Get comfortable with the steps.

Secret #33: The key to winning the "salary expectations game" is to keep the ball in the interviewer's court.

Secret #34: Being too flexible can depreciate your candidacy.

Secret #35: Make your employment decision based on the opportunity, not personalities.

Secret #36: In salary negotiations, he who speaks first often loses.

Secret #37: Negotiating for pennies can cost you a bundle.

Secret #38: Get the offer in writing before tendering your resignation.

Secret #39: Negotiate advance notice of termination or compensation in lieu of notice.

Secret #40: Accepting a counteroffer can mean a slow death for your career.

Secret #41: Negotiate extended temporary housing allowance.

Secret #42: Your earliest battles should be those that are easiest to win.

Secret #43: The best time to consider other opportunities is when you're happy where you are.

Secret #44: Establish yourself as an industry expert.

Secret #45: Develop ongoing relationships with search consultants.

Secret #46: Be courteous to the headhunter. The next head hunted may be your own!

INDEX